The Year of the Child

BEL MOONEY

The Year of the Child

Hutchinson of London

For E. M. and G. M.
with love from their child

Hutchinson & Co. (Publishers) Ltd
3 Fitzroy Square, London, London W1P 6JD

London Melbourne Sydney Auckland
Wellington Johannesburg and agencies
throughout the world

First published 1979

© Bel Mooney 1979

Set in VIP Garamond
Printed in Great Britain by The Anchor Press Ltd
and bound by Wm Brendon & Son Ltd,
both of Tiptree, Essex

British Library CIP data

Mooney, Bel
    The year of the child.
    1. Child psychology – Case studies
    2. Child development – Great Britain – Case
    studies
    I. Title
    155.4′092′6   BF721

ISBN 0 09 138320 X (cased)
        0 09 138321 8 (paper)

Contents

Acknowledgements

Obviously I owe everything to the families who allowed me to enter their lives. Two chose to have their surnames omitted, for reasons of privacy, and I myself took the decision to disguise the identity of the family in Chapter 7. I am also grateful to all the schools mentioned in the book for permitting me to sit in lesson after lesson for days.

I want to thank the South London Hospital and the Borough of Sunderland for their co-operation, and the following 'scouts' for help and sometimes hospitality: Vivien Womersley, James Hunte, Thelma McGough, Jane Hutt, Brian and Helen Walker, Bert Beaumont, Arthur and Ann Scargill, Stuart Foster, John Hambley, Jimmy Boyle, and Ken Murray.

Without patient transcription and typing by Susan Simmons and Phillipa Jury (our visiting New Zealander who had to struggle with English accents) this book would never have been completed. Thanks to J for his encouragement. And there is a special extra debt to Daniel, who actually managed not to resent that fact that I cared about other peoples' children as well as my own.

All photographs by Bel Mooney.

He lives in his childhood. He must be observed rather than analysed
... in an endeavour to ascertain the conflict through which he
passes in his relations with grown-up persons and with his social
environment. It is clear that this approach will lead us away from
psycho-analytic theories and technique into a new field of observa-
tion of the child in his social existence.

MARIA MONTESSORI The Secret of Childhood (1936)

BORN YESTERDAY

Tightly-folded bud,
I have wished you something
None of the others would:
Not the usual stuff
About being beautiful
Or running off a spring
Of innocence and love —
They will all wish you that,
And should it prove possible,
Well, you're a lucky girl.

But if it shouldn't, then
May you be ordinary;
Have, like other women,
An average of talents:
Not ugly, not good-looking,
Nothing uncustomary
To pull you off your balance,
That, unworkable itself,
Stops all the rest from working.
In fact, may you be dull —
If that is what a skilled,
Vigilant, flexible,
Unemphasised, enthralled
Catching of happiness is called.

PHILIP LARKIN

Introduction

Once, I asked a five-year-old what he wanted to be when he grows up. A train driver, I guessed, or a soldier, a sailor, or a sweet-shop man. He did not hesitate. 'A daddy,' he replied, 'because you *have* to be a daddy.' In that second the future unfolded: the repetitive pattern most of us scribble on our own clean slates. The tiny child watches, absorbs what is around him, grows, and usually imitates in words and deed what he has seen. At the age of three the little girl mirrors her mother's gestures. By ten the boy estimates his future according to the measurements he has learnt. They grow older; they leave school and childhood behind, usually heading surely towards a re-enactment of the same process: to produce another small soul who will one day say that, yes, he *must* be a daddy.

As this book progressed, the cycle became all the more obvious. A truism it may be – a Wordsworthian as well as a Freudian perception – but it surprised me nevertheless that I should start by being committed to a book about children as individuals, and end by seeing them all (despite their very different backgrounds) as united by near-helplessness in the face of the forces that surround them. Of course there are some children who break away: who leave their mining villages to become successful playwrights, or who bring disgrace to their public school by ending up in prison. But those are the exceptions. My intention was to write about those children who are not exceptional, or, rather, who do not seem so. The book is intended as a celebration of ordinariness.

People do not, as a rule, consider their own lives to be worthy of any study, nor would they agree with Yevtushenko's words:

> No people are uninteresting,
> Their fate is like the chronicles of planets.

The mother of one of the children in this book sat in a Cardiff club and said: 'I hope you've found something out that interests you, because I can't see what could possibly be interesting to anybody in our life. My first husband died, and my second husband beat me up and I've got four ordinary kids. Who could possibly be interested in that?'

Another mother, from a very different social background, wrote and said, 'I am afraid we are very dull and ordinary parents.' It is never the case. On a train journey, frozen for a moment in the frame of the speeding window, you can see a woman hanging out washing in one back garden, a man mending something, a hooded pram in a yard, a boy kicking a ball, an old man with his hand on the fence, and know that within each house is being unfolded a small and passionate drama of everyday life. It is that sense that I set out to convey in these chapters: the conviction that whatever happens matters.

What happens does not happen just to the child in isolation. It is too easy to get articulate older children to talk into a tape-recorder; what I wanted to do was write about the whole lives (as much as possible) of children who are not articulate, and of their families – at a certain point in time. Maria Montessori wrote: '. . . whether we go to the origins of human life, or follow the child in his work of growth, we always find the adult not far away. The life of a child is a line joining two adult generations. The child's life, which creates and is being created, starts in one adult and ends in another adult. It is the lane along which he passes, skirting closely the lives of adults, and the study of it brings fresh rewards of interest and light.' In this book (particularly in the early chapters) as well as observing children we hear the voices of adults, because it is they who are shaping the children's lives, at school and at home.

But what sort of 'study'? I am not a sociologist nor a psychologist: the form of this book is straightforwardly journalistic. During one year I spent time with twelve families, from twelve different parts of the British Isles, moving on as the months passed. There are four sections in the book, as there are four seasons in the year – each one representing both the season itself, and the stage of development of the children. Spring is the time of growth and hope, from birth to four or five, when the child's world is that of the home, when he/she is surrounded by voices but cannot speak for himself. Summer is the time of flowering – between the ages of five and eight, when most teachers will confirm that children are outgoing and loving, forming friendships quickly, and coming for the first time under the influence of adults who are not family. Autumn is the third stage, representing not so much a dying as a cooling, taking the child from nine to thirteen – a difficult time of change. Children start to worry, about school, friends, themselves, ceasing to be as confident and starting to form their own judgements. Winter is the teenage years, when the world exerts its pressures: exams, sex, parents, what people think, what to do, what to be. . . . The child has to cope, for the first time, with the knowledge that he or she is getting older, growing up. The book starts with the birth of a baby, and ends with a boy who is sixteen and has left school – whose childhood has ended, and who can speak for himself.

The twelve children in the book represent as accurate a cross-section of British kids as one could get – without the sociologists' samples, studies and statistics. I chose them randomly, in that whichever child I found was the right one, since articulacy or special talent or confidence were not criteria that mattered at all. I do not make comparisons, but so that it is possible for them to be made, I chose the children from three social groups. Market research categories are simplistic and often misleading, since class cannot be defined purely by income, but the three groups divide roughly as follows:

(1) unskilled and semi-skilled working class;
(2) skilled working class and lower middle class;
(3) professional middle class.

In each of the four sections there is one child from each group, so that, although the children are separate and unique individuals, the shared threads of differing opportunity and expectancy run through the whole narrative. Types they are not; typical they are.

This book is not, though, simply about individuals at a particular moment in their lives, it is also about growth, development, change. I see the 'year' of the title as the state of childhood itself: a dog has its day and a child has its 'year', and when it is over it is gone forever. Each stage does symbolize a loss, although I would not be sentimental enough to dwell on this at the expense of an appreciation of the gains. Most parents spend their time vacillating between two emotions: the desire to see their children at the next stage – walking, talking, reading, playing in the school football team, going to the first disco – and the impossible wish that they could stay where they are. More than one parent used the word 'innocent'. As I talked to all these children, and to their friends and families, the experience did crystallize into what seemed to be an exploration of that loss of innocence which is at the root of human experience. Innocence may be a fantasy, yet like all myths it is imaginatively essential, and carries with it the need to generate the next generation, and the next, to see the whole process happen again.

It is not a process which I see as sad. Though winter may be bleak, the seeds of knowledge and understanding lie beneath the surface. What they produce may be understandable anger, it may be predictable success, or it may simply be the sort of acceptance expressed by Philip Larkin at the end of 'Coming':

> It will be spring soon,
> It will be spring soon –
> As I whose childhood
> Is a forgotten boredom,
> Feel like a child
> Who comes on a scene
> Of adult reconciling,
> And can understand nothing
> But the unusual laughter,
> And starts to be happy.

Spring

1 Denise

It was snowing. Joan Robertson sat in the smart sitting room of her comfortable council house in Southfields, in the heart of a character-less area of South London, bored, looking out at the blizzard. Gary and Tracy, thirteen and twelve, were at their comprehensive school, Kim, who is ten, was at the special school for spina bifida children in Putney. There is nothing to do when you are expecting a child, except wait, and worry – especially in the light of the past. So the first slow cold months of the year were swallowed by the waiting, with the visits to the clinic the only thing Joan could look forward to, because they at least made the whole thing more real.

Geoff dropped her off at the South London Hospital for Women, an imposing red-brick pile opposite Clapham Common. Joan joined the thirty or so women sitting in rows in the small, aptly named waiting room, muttering, 'It takes *ages*.' The women's faces were blank; they sat with arms crossed loosely across their swollen stomachs, waiting for their names to be called. Mrs Ahmed, Mrs Ngosi, Mrs Brown: they each shuffled in their unbalanced way across to the scales, removing their shoes, gazing uncomprehendingly at the mysterious kilos, sitting again, waiting to be summoned through to the cubicle area. There more women sat in rows, some wearing dressing gowns, with the blank patient look of people who have grown used to time.

After one and three-quarter hours Joan is called. She heaves her-self up on to the bed, baring her arm for the nurse to take her blood pressure. The woman, who is plump, jolly and in her mid-forties, looks at Joan. 'Have you been resting?'

'Why? Is it up?'

'Yes, a little. I'd prefer it down a bit – but you've always had a problem with the blood pressure, haven't you? Mind, it could be something to do with the sitting waiting out there.'

Joan nods and sighs: 'Yes, it can be frustrating.'

Nurse smiles, '24th March, is it?'

'Yes.'

'Another four weeks! Any complaints?'

'It's still moving a lot. I think he's going to be a footballer.'

'Well, you're an old hand at this game, you should know what to expect.'

'Yes, but it's so long since the others that I've forgotten.'

Dr Vedivathi, the registrar, rustles into the room in a saffron sari, looks at the notes, then feels Joan's abdomen. The stomach looks impossibly swollen, white with a tracery of fine purple lines, and bluish mottling, so stretched that it might burst when the black ear trumpet is pressed into the skin.

The doctor listens – hears the tiny impatient throb of the foetal heart. Her brown hands press Joan's flesh, Joan's own hands following. 'What's that bit there?' she asks. 'Is it his shoulder?'

'No, it's the head, look, you can feel it. And the shoulder is there, and the feet there.'

'My husband says it's going to be a boy.'

Joan complains that she has been feeling sick, despite her diet of 'plenty of fish, greens, protein'. But it is one of the unpleasant aspects of pregnancy the staff expect, so they say little.

That night, the children come home from school to find their mother sitting listlessly watching television, still feeling sick. Tracy longs for the baby to come because she wants to take it out in its pram. Gary appears to be indifferent, but wrote, 'The baby is going to be a boy' all over the about-to-be-decorated wall upstairs. Kim arrives in the special bus from the spina bifida school and walks unevenly into the room, leaning heavily on her sticks. Her face is bright and pretty, with fair hair curling on her cheeks. She asks, 'How's Fred?' using the friendly name they have already given to the foetus inside Joan's womb.

'He's fine.'

Kim sits on the floor, laying her sticks beside her: 'I hope he's not moving about too much and kicking you.'

'Oh, he's always moving, Kim.'

'Well, if he hurts you I'll bash him one.' She clenches her fist and grins. 'Anyway, I hope he won't scream too much at night and keep me awake.'

'All babies cry and keep you awake.'

Kim is turning the pages of the mother-and-baby magazines on the coffee table. She holds up a picture of a baby being born, and Tracy says, 'Ugh, I've seen that on TV – it's horrible, with all the blood spurting out. I'd rather see a baby in its clothes.'

But Kim points to a photograph of the mother holding the newborn child, the father smiling gently. 'Oh, I think that's *lovely*.'

Joan Robertson is thirty three, with shoulder-length blonde hair framing a round face. She married Geoffrey when she was nineteen and he was twenty, when they had worked together for nine months at a television rental firm in South London. She was a supervisor in the service department, and he was a television engineer.

'Well, we always wanted to have four children, that was our aim. But after having Kim, and the shock of that, we decided that was it, we didn't want any more. But you know, I am one of four . . . and I just thought it would be nice to even it up. Geoff took a lot of convincing – that I would be able to have these tests, and that if this baby was spina bifida it would show in the tests. Even though we'd had the tests there was still a slight possibility that we could have another spina bifida baby.' She grimaces, and rubs her stomach. 'So now I keep thinking, *Is* that his feet I feel moving?

'Before we got married his mum said that Geoff wasn't over-keen on children. And when I mentioned it to him he said, I don't know – but I wouldn't want them for a while. But after we'd got married, the first thing we wanted was to have a baby. I don't know why you feel like that. I suppose it's an extension of your love for one another, to have a child. We got married in September and Gary was born in July the following year. We had an unfurnished flat; we were quite happy with what we had. But I'd made my mind up before not to let the babies take over. When we went to our friends and there was baby clothes all over, and everything stood for Baby, with toys and nappies hanging about, I thought, no. Although I wanted a baby I said I wouldn't let it interfere with my life like that. I had Gary, then Tracy a year later, and it was a lot of work, but as soon as Geoff came home I used to devote my time to him. We'd always have those few hours to ourselves, even after Kim. I think it's important. People may laugh, but husbands *do* get jealous, the children are getting all your attention, and not them.

'It must have been just after Christmas last year that I decided. I was working at the South London Hospital taking blood samples – and that didn't help, going on the maternity wards, thinking, Aren't those babies lovely? Kim was mad about babies. We'd take her out in the wheelchair, and she'd see a baby in a pram and say, Oh, Mummy, look at that baby. Why can't we have one? And Geoff and I would look at each other. It's a funny urge . . . this maternal instinct. It comes and goes. I used to see friends with babies and feel nothing. Then I'd think I'd love a baby. Then the feeling goes away and you think no more of it. But with me, the last few months before we decided, yes, we'll have another baby, the feeling grew stronger and stronger, and it wouldn't go away. And of course, knowing that I could have the tests gave me greater hope that this baby would be . . . well, as perfect . . . as it could be. I don't suppose, to be honest, we thought about the first three babies. But after having Kim, it makes you think hard. So you know what you're doing. With the others Geoff just dropped me off at the hospital and came back when it was all over. But with this one he wants to be present at the delivery. He seems more involved – like going and getting a cot – he'd never have done that! It's being that much more mature. But you know, I think we're going to worry more about this baby – being older. When we were that young we just got on with it!'

As February passed into March the weather grew colder. The waiting room at the hospital seemed fuller each time, the women all the more cumbersome for the weight of their damp coats, woollen hats and scarves.

On 17th March 140 women passed through the ante-natal clinic, all waiting for their babies. Joan took her place, but only had to wait for half an hour this time before she was called.

The consultant, Miss Sibthorp, looking like a kindly primary school headmistress, examines Joan. Blood pressure down; still too heavy, for despite her recurring sickness she cannot lose weight; baby moving constantly, punching and pushing through her flesh.

Miss Sibthorp says that there will be no clinic the next Friday – Good Friday, when the baby is due. But if Joan does not go into labour during Easter, they will induce immediately afterwards, sparing her more waiting. She smiles with relief.

At school, Tracy daydreams about the baby, looking out of the window, guessing that it *must* be a boy, hearing her teacher tell her sharply to get on with the work. The day before, her teacher had set the class to write an essay about Easter. In large round letters she wrote:

I like Easter best because of the eggs. It is a very happy moment for people because my mum is having a baby. I want a baby boy because girls get on the nerves they are very messy. But it will be a very happy moment for my mum. I think it will be one of the happiest days of her life. I can't wait to take the baby out in his or her pram. . . . That is why I am going to enjoy Easter.

In the comfortable, gold-coloured sitting room she and her mother indulge themselves, poring over *Book of Life* issues on conception and childbirth.

Joan says: 'To me it's just a thing that moves. I won't let myself imagine it. I've got the cot and everything waiting up there, but I won't let myself think about when it's born. It's not a baby. I can feel it but I can't imagine it. It's just a thing inside my swelling belly. Not a baby. It moves, so I know it's there. Until I see it as a baby in my arms, I don't want to think too much. I admit I'm afraid.'

Each day throughout her pregnancy Joan has risen at seven o'clock, woken up her disabled daughter Kim, taken her to the bathroom, washed her, changed her nappy, powdered her, and helped her dress. Then Geoff takes over, giving the children breakfast and putting Kim on the coach which takes her to school, whilst Joan rests in bed, waiting for the sharp morning kicks. Geoff does not leave for work until lunch-time, then works until about midnight, driving a heavy goods vehicle for a dairy in North London. He is tall and good-natured, with a quick temper his children have learned to know.

'I left school at fifteen, I was never good at school. Looking back, that's one thing I regret – I mean, what's always let me down is reading and writing and things like that, though I can do anything with a car. I mend cars as a sideline for a bit of extra cash. Look at me – I earn a hundred pounds a week for driving a lorry. Now Gary, he's interested in history, but what's the point? There's no point in learning these days. All you're going to have to do is push a button. Though sometimes I wonder if I might have done better if I'd learnt more . . . . I floated about a good deal after I left school, even went in the army for about a year. I didn't reckon me time there – I was in the wrong mob to start with. I was in the Grenadier Guards, when I wanted to be on the mechanical side. Didn't like the toy soldier business – all the tourists coming and screwing you with their cameras. I jumped the wall a couple of times and came home and got taken back, but eventually they kicked me out on medical grounds.

'Joan always left it up to me what I did. I mean, I *have* come unstuck sometimes, and Joan's known that was going to happen, and she was right. I mean, Joan's got her head screwed on right. I don't mind telling you I think the world of Joan. I love bringing her something home as a surprise. . . . I like giving her those cuddly toys: she's got a wardrobe upstairs with loads of them on top. I know it sounds silly, but I know what her face will be like when I give it

to her. I suppose over the fourteen years of marriage we've had our
ups and our downs, but my marriage has been brought closer
together with having Kim.

'As soon as we got married we wanted children. It was the 'in'
thing. That's what brings marriage together – kids. Without them
your marriage isn't as close. You centre your work around bringing
up your children – it gives you a sense of values. I like it. Anyway,
we had Gary and Tracy very close together, and went on and had
Kim, because we wanted four. Well, Joan was in the delivery room,
and I'd come up, and the baby was on the other side of the door, and
they said, Sorry, the baby's got to go away for an operation. I said,
What's wrong with it? I want to *know*. They said that it was spina
bifida and I said, What the bloody hell is that? I hadn't got a clue.
Joan had seen a TV programme so she knew more than me.

'I think for the first twelve months we just couldn't accept that
our child was disabled. I don't think I blamed Joan, and I don't
think Joan blamed me, but it was always at the back of our minds
that something between me and Joan wasn't right. That it was
something . . . *we* had *done* – but it wasn't. It was just a freak of
nature. It happened, and that's it, and you've both got to come to
live with the idea that you've got a disabled child, and carry on
living the same as normal. It's not normal, mind, and there is a
great deal of strain.

'So I never look to the future. I live from day to day. We don't
worry about money: if we've got it we've got it, if we haven't we
wait till we have. I mean, I work as hard as I can to get us every little
luxury possible. All right, I've got a council house, but it doesn't
worry me. I couldn't care two monkeys what people think. I'd like
to own me own house, and when I've got the money to afford it I
will, but until then I'll stay with the council. My kids have got
everything they want – Tracy and Gary have got portable televisions
in their bedrooms, and I never had that, but I wanted my kids to
have it. I had a second-hand pushbike, I wanted Gary and Tracy to
have brand-new bikes. But they respect things. I'm strict with them
– I won't accept no cheek. I was brought up strict and I knew it
would rub off on my children, which it has. If you bring them up
like that then you'll find your children will help you and respect you
– which mine do. My children will always help Joan out, if I say
something they'll go and do it. There'll be a little bit of argument,
but you get over that. They're good kids. So with them growing up
now, and me getting a good wage, we thought we could manage
four. That was our intention all along.

'Sometimes I worry. Obviously Joan and I are very worried about this baby – whether it will be normal, though we don't talk about it. We don't like to. But I'm worried. I'm very worried. And I worry in the respect of what the world will be like when it's about ten years old, what changes there will be in the world. As I said, you can't plan. People are changing all the time – you get older, and wiser, and tighter. So you think, what's it going to be like in ten years' time? Is it [the baby] going to walk round the corner and see four Pakis to one white? Don't get me wrong, I'm not colour prejudiced, I think Africans are good workers, but I'm prejudiced against Pakis. Because it's pushing English people not to have any more children – and the way I look at it, we've always been looked up to in the past. This used to be a great country; we don't walk round with guns in our pockets like the Americans. But it's getting like that. Look at football matches.

'You know what it all comes back to? The upbringing of the child. People don't *think*. I detest seeing prams outside a pub, and mum and dad are in there swigging it back. I can't stand that. If I go to a pub where there is a garden, then I'll take the kids, and I'll bring the booze outside. They can be *with* you. They've got some part of your life; and they think it's good to be sitting there out with mum and dad. Terrific, they're eating their crisps and loving it, because they're part of *you*. This is what life's all about. If you can involve your children in your life, they're on top – they are doing what mum and dad are doing, and they can go to school and tell their mates they went to the pub with mum and dad and sat in the garden. I think that is what everybody should do with their kids. They should get up, and look at the way they're bringing them up. Because this country could be a beautiful country – it *could* – if the people that live in it would only think about what they're doing – and about their kids.'

Good Friday came quietly, and the family sat at home, waiting for the drama. Joan kept feeling twinges, but they would pass, leaving the unseen baby kicking strongly as before, as if it, too, was growing impatient. Shopping on Saturday, Easter eggs, Sunday lunch, the almost-boring silence of the cold Bank Holiday Monday with the children still talking about 'Fred', guessing that it will be a boy, saying they positively do not want a girl, and Joan listening, feeling nervy, wishing it was over. She felt depressed – her whole being concentrated upon that centre point where the baby stirred ceaselessly, and her own sick nervous flutters accompanied its movement.

Joan's case is already packed. Although she knows there is a controversy about inductions she feels nothing but relief. It will soon be over. In the last few days her fears about the baby have grown.

At two o'clock on 28th March Geoff delivers her to the hospital, leaving her to be shaved, given an enema, and told they would be breaking the waters at 5 p.m. She feels surprised, and slightly afraid, because she thought they would wait until the next day.

She lies alone in the labour ward, looking at the shiny ceiling, listening to distant noises of crying babies, and waiting for the grip of the pain, muted at first, then increasing in intensity. Echoes. Shifting her head from side to side. Surprised by the speed, as contraction follows contraction ... calling.

At 7 p.m. Geoff arrives to find his wife in the last stages of labour, sleepy with pethidine, being wheeled into the delivery room. Nurses rush about donning their white caps and paper face masks, and the necessary gloves. He stares. 'I'm bottling out,' he says, suddenly afraid, and takes his seat in the waiting room.

Joan is waxy pale, lying behind her own belly, knees apart, revealed – utterly vulnerable. Nurse Spense is quickly tying the ribbons behind her own gown, Sister Anderson and Sister Kossine stand each side of Joan, who grips her own thighs. She asks in a small voice if she can push. Yes. She does so heavily, with a small grunt.

Then, 'Can I push again please?' She sounds like a schoolgirl asking for a favour.

'Yes,' says one of the sisters, through her mask, 'just a little push, a little one. That's it. Stop.' Despite the urgency the room seems silent and very, very still. In the centre, through the bruised petals of an opening flower, the dark patch of head, tiny, moist, then bigger.

'Another push, Joan – yes, that's right, and now pant. Pant, Joan.' The voice is raised. Joan starts to pant, then laughs silently.

'Oh, you lost it, Joan, you started fine. Now pant, again ... now again, a little push.'

The instructions are excited; expert hands are finding the head, easing it, turning it. As Joan grunts, her head lolling to one side, her eyes squeezed shut, the face of her child appears, its tiny eyes also closed, its face squashed with the strain they share, this struggle into separate existence. Mouth, neck, shoulders hunched — as Joan lets out another heavy breath, the baby slithers out, trailing its long, blue-grey, glutinous cord of life. The tiny arms and legs are blue and shiny, the head almost purple, streaked with white and fresh red blood.

'Yes, *yes!*' the staff are crying out, 'well done.' For a second there is silence — but when the cord is cut, and Joan's child is severed from her, the first tiny cry is heard. She looks to one side, a terrible anxiety in her face. 'Is it all right? *Is* it?' she whispers. It is a perfect baby girl.

'That was quick, Joan ... you're a speedy worker,' laughs Sister Anderson, as Sister Kossine wraps the baby in a green cloth and lays her against Joan's cheek. Dark hair, the face turning fresh pink from the purple, the eyes opening darkest blue and looking at the blur of white and light, feeling this warm mother's flesh for the first time and hearing the echoing noises, the clatter, the talk — far now from that throbbing darkness, the safety of the nine months' union. Then taken, wrapped in a white blanket, deposited in a perspex cot, already feeling unfamiliar pangs of hunger. Her tiny face stares through the side, like a fish in a bowl, whilst her tiny fingers with their transparent nails push at the blanket.

'Thank God,' says Geoff. Everything is all right — a perfect baby. He stands in a white hat and gown, the huge man cradling the baby, grinning widely down at her. 'Isn't she lovely? Isn't she? Well, it's Denise. Hello, Denise.'

'We didn't have a Fred, we had a Freda,' smiles Joan wearily from the bed. 'Three girls and a boy. Gary will be disappointed.'

'Lucky we had two names. Hey, you're heavy, a real weight.'

'Imagine what it's like carrying all that inside you.'

Geoff is still staring down. 'I wonder what you'll be. Can't be a footballer now.'

'Oh, I don't know — what about women's liberation?' Joan smiles at them both.

Joan is almost dropping off to sleep — the pethidine is having its effect. 'It's funny, I can't believe it's over. It's a sort of anticlimax, after all that waiting. I wouldn't swop her for the world, though.'

Denise still struggles inside the blanket. Geoff leans over to pat her: 'Welcome to the world. I hope there'll be a world left by the time you grow up. I'll go home now, Joan, and make me phone calls. Do you want me to bring anything tomorrow?'

'Just bring yourself.' She smiles.

Left alone. The midwives have already cleared up. It is over.

Kim cried when she heard. Tracy rang relatives, but Gary carried on with his jigsaw, concentrating on the difficult, shapeless mass of the trees. Underneath the excitement, the house seemed empty without Joan, lacking its centre. Geoff rang his friends, then sat down with a drink to celebrate, telling Tracy about the baby: 'We've got to learn to call her Denise, now.'

'I knew it wouldn't have spina bifida, it was kicking too much,' said Tracy.

Geoff nodded. 'You see, we was *all* worried, though nobody said.'

'I can't wait to see her,' said Tracy. 'I can't wait to take her out in the pram. And mum will be back to normal again, back to her usual self.'

Denise was taken away, weighed, washed, and put to sleep in the nursery with the other babies. She was checked at 7.30 p.m., then every hour until six o'clock the next morning, nurses noting that her respiration, colour of skin, vomit and cord were all 'satisfactory'. In the cool grey morning light she was given to her mother to feed, fastening on to the nipple immediately and sucking hard, tiny hands clawing at the white and blue-veined mountain of flesh. She smelt her mother's skin. Her whole body moved almost imperceptibly to the rhythm of her sucking. It was the 29th of March, the first full day of her life.

Later, the small room is filled with sunlight. In one bed a dark-haired girl lies silently cradling her baby. In the other Joan Robertson lies huddled asleep, blonde hair tousled, her back to the door. Denise sleeps under a pink blanket beside the bed. There is a perpetual sound of distant mewling; a smell of boiled potatoes permeates the green lino and shiny yellow walls. Outside a brisk wind buffets clouds across the sky, chasing sudden shadows outside the silent room.

Voices outside. The family have arrived to see the baby. Kim hurries on her metal sticks, Tracy rushes ahead. They both hang over the cot saying Ooooh! and Aaaah! whilst Gary stalks to the opposite end of the bed and peers from a safe distance. The children give their mother a huge padded card, explaining that they put their money together; Geoff and his sister Yvonne give her cards and knitted cardigans, telling her who phoned, what they said. Joan hardly seems to notice but sits placidly in the middle of the fuss, hoping they won't wake Denise. Tracy looks crossly from the cot, telling Gary that he should at least *look* at his new sister. Ten minutes later, embarrassed, the tall gangly boy saunters over – then does not leave the cot for the rest of the hour. The three children surround it, exclaiming over her hair, her tiny fingernails, her wrinkled ears. They give her a black and white panda, putting it gently at her feet.

Tracy: 'She's got her face all screwed up.'

Joan: 'How can you blame her – with your great face staring down at her?'

Tracy: 'She's got such a little nose.'

Gary: 'You've got a little nose, Tracy.'

Tracy: 'Hasn't she got thick lips?'

Gary (looking up with the air of one who has made a great discovery): 'She's cute – *cute*!'

Kim: 'I thought she'd have long black hair. But it's short.'

The adults are discussing arrangements: Geoff's shifts make it difficult to ensure that Joan will have help when she first arrives home. Yvonne makes suggestions – but the children ignore these adult concerns.

Kim: 'Can you see her little tongue? Can you see her little feet?'

Joan: 'They think she's a little doll.'

Geoff: 'That's what I said they'd be like. Stop touching her! She's not a toy. You won't be making a fuss of her when she's crying at home, you'll be running a mile.'

Yvonne: 'You wait till they've had enough of her, Joan. I'll give it a week.'

Geoff: 'Look, you lot, *leave . . . her . . . ALONE!*'

Tracy (tossing her head): 'She's *my* sister.'

Kim (indignantly): 'It's *our* baby.'

Geoff: 'No, it's not – it's mine.'

Yvonne reminds Geoff that he had said that if the baby turned out to be a girl he would dump it on her doorstep. He looks ashamed. 'Oh, *she's* all right.'

Joan asks if they are happy with her, and Kim and Tracy cry, 'Oh, yes,' whilst Gary says, 'She'll do.' Tracy and Kim squabble over who will hold her.

Gary: 'When I'm twenty one how old will she be?' He pauses to calculate. 'Eight, yes, eight.'

Tracy passes Denise to Kim, worrying about the loose and fragile head, whilst the voices babble on around – placing Denise forever within her family, claiming her as their own.

When they have gone, Joan sits looking at the dark eyes, the cracked skin. 'It's all right, they've gone now. You can relax, Denise.'

On Friday, 7th April, Denise went out for the first time in her new pram – a low-slung, dark blue Silver Cross, gleaming with chrome. A week ago Geoff went to collect it, after he had brought Joan home to the flowers and cards and congratulations. Joan had told him she had paid £10 off a £70 pram. But he discovered there was £75 owing, and paid it with good humour. Nothing is too good, or too much . . . or too dull. In the first week of Denise Robertson's life, she did not know that five people exclaimed over her every sound, noted her burps and laughed when she evacuated noisily into her nappy, a look of concentration on her face. Five people discussed her features, whom she looked like, what she would be.

And then, when it seemed that spring had come at last, after the snow and the wind, the five people wrapped her in white wool, placed her gently in her new carriage, and took her out to show the world. Gary pushed the pram out of the door, Geoff steered it up the path, Joan pushed it a little way along the road, then Tracy took over possessively, though afraid of the kerbs. They thought people were looking at them. The world for Denise was a bright cold mass of light, outside the tight darkness of the pram – a strange bumping, with noises of cars, birds, voices, and the hum all round of the city.

At home, Joan changed her nappy. 'I'm not at all disappointed – that she's a girl. I wasn't, anyway, and then today I looked at the little clothes in Mothercare, little dresses with matching pants and scarves, and I thought you can dress up little girls much better than little boys. Prettier. And the kids are thrilled, all they want to do is play with her and take her out. But I suppose they'll get fed up. In a year's time I'll be begging them, and they won't want to know.'

Kim examined Denise's leg. 'I won't. I'll look after her forever.'

2 Mandy

Early morning, the blue hour before the milkman rattles bottles on the step, even before the child's first murmur. Ray Green hears his alarm at five thirty, switches it off, turns over, then slowly, unwillingly, pulls himself from the bed, tiptoes past the cot, and goes out to the cold bathroom to wash. He shivers into his overalls, prepares his haversack for work, then goes into the kitchen to prepare Mandy's breakfast bottle, carefully measuring her medicine, Calciferol, into the milk. By this time she may be awake, lying in the cot, smiling up at the grey ceiling. Barbara still huddles asleep, so Ray gives the child the bottle, and then sits in the living room from about six-twenty until six forty-five reading a war paperback. Then he walks out, joins the other men in donkey jackets and jeans at the bus-stop, and makes the familiar journey to work, through the sprawling estates on the outskirts, and on to the centre of Sunderland.

Once he has clocked on he prepares his Daf pickup for the day, checking the oil and water. It was a major disappointment when a new Bedford was not allocated to him, as he had expected. Each day the routine is the same: the block of shops in Pennywell, and then the estate itself, meeting the same people, sharing the same jokes. 'I'm just a sweeper, that's all. A driver-sweeper. Street orderly I think is the posh name for it!'

Ray Green notices the people who drop papers where he has swept; he answers the calls of distress from elderly ladies whose dogs have died, and lie perhaps in the back garden – moving with maggots – and still mourned. He clears up, wrinkling his nose, and as he works he thinks about Claire and Mandy. It is silly, he confesses, but he has an obsession about Mandy being dropped, and a sudden vision of her plump little body crashing down to the floor will make him rush into a call box and ring home, just to be sure. At one o'clock he will look at his watch and remember that Claire will be on her way to nursery school, and after three the glances at his wrist bring him nearer the time when he can rush for the early bus. He says he cannot cut off from his family when he is at work.

Ray Green is one of 520 men who work at the Beach Street depot in Sunderland. When he gets off the bus at his stop in the Downhill Estate he walks home to one of 1109 council properties – small, identical houses and maisonettes that were built about fourteen years ago. The estate is pleasant, though bleak, with its windy stretches of turf unmarred by swings or slides. There is a workmen's club, where Ray sometimes joins his father and his brother Alan for a drink. Alan works on the buses; Mr Green, who is in his sixties, teaches youths painting and decorating as part of the job creation scheme. They live nearby, with Ray's mother and Alan's wife and two children, temporarily in one house. Ray is close to his family.

Past the club, along the road, then he turns into Kinsale Square, walking along the 'backs' to his maisonette. It is a short cul-de-sac, with garages at the end scarred by graffiti. Ray does not have a car – in fact, only one third of the families in Sunderland have a car, which explains the disused air of those garages. Up the steps, passing the front door of the childless couple who live immediately beneath them, and who have stopped speaking to the Greens because of the noise the children make, and then Ray opens his own front door. He walks down the short dark hall, knowing what will happen as soon as he opens the living room door.

Claire shrieks and falls upon him, and Mandy sits in her pushchair in the corner, stretching out her arms, begging to be picked up. Their cries rival; each laments the louder if he picks up the other. He gives them the sweets he brings home each night, but Ray knows that there will be no respite, no time for him to take off his overalls even, until he stands holding them both, Claire and Mandy, in front of the crackling fire.

'It makes me feel a bit chuffed actually – pleased, like. You feel, at least they know us. I'm no stranger. I'd like to sit down and unwind with a cup of tea and a fag, just for half an hour, without the bairns, but there's no chance. I'm through that door, attacked from all sides. But I wouldn't have it different.'

Barbara and Ray Green have been married for seven years, the last two of which they have spent in the tiny, £8.15 a week, two-bedroom flat. Ray is thirty one, Barbara is twenty seven, and they married after meeting in a pub in Barbara's home town in Yorkshire. They used to sit and plan their white wedding, talking about the children they would have. There was no question of it – though Ray wanted about ten, and Barbara thought one would be enough. He would say that to have one would not be fair: the child would be lonely, would need a playmate. So if two, why not three? They are still discussing it. One thing Ray was sure of – he only wanted daughters, and he knew that he would indulge them. He used to say to Barbara even then that if they wanted something they would only have to come to him and they would get it.

It is mid-morning in Ray's small flat; Mandy (in a yellow Babygro) is sitting in her pushchair next to the television set, which is showing an old Terry Thomas film. She ignores the programme, only occasionally turning her head to gaze at the flickering grey image, about eighteen inches away. Claire too shows no interest, walking around and stamping her feet to the imaginary tunes of her two-string plastic guitar. Claire is four years old, Mandy eighteen months.

Outside, a grey sky and freezing wind do not encourage expeditions, even if there was somewhere to play on the estate. Tonight snow will fall again, even sweeping south, carrying with it news images of smashed and stranded cars, and newborn spring lambs dying in Scotland. A bright coal fire cheers the small room.

'Book! Claire's book! *Claire*'s. . . .' The demands continue until Barbara takes the thick catalogue from its box, and sits her eldest daughter on the settee, with a warning not to tear the pages. Claire stares at the clothes, the stereos, the jewellery, the continental quilts and knick-knacks that fill the pages – all available on easy terms. The child is fascinated; the 'book' halts her habitual progress around the room as even children's television cannot. 'Look, Mandy,' she cries, pointing to a picture of a wendy house. But Mandy cannot see, sitting in the pushchair, examining her feet. Then there is a picture of a lawnmower surrounded by flowers. It excites her: 'Look Mandy, Mandy! Flowers. Nice flowers.'

Most mornings are spent like this: Mandy watching Claire, Barbara doing her housework, the television on. Before lunch they go to the shops, to buy that day's food. The shopping takes Barbara from the house, although she does not chat much to the shop assistants, content that the man in the greengrocer's always gives Claire a piece of fruit.

Preparing for the exodus takes time: the children are dressed in coats and bonnets, and Mandy is laced into special boots they have just received from the Department of Health and Social Security. When she was a year old they discovered that she had a calcium deficiency, which means that she finds it hard to walk or crawl because her bones are too soft. So the special blue leather boots will support her ankles – and Barbara smiles: 'Do you know, these would cost about £60 if you had to pay for them. I think they're great.'

Mandy's new bonnet cost only 50p from a friend and Barbara puts the coat hood up as well, explaining that as Mandy has suffered from a bad chest, she worries about the cold. At last they are ready, and Claire rushes on whilst Barbara laboriously bumps the pushchair down the stone stairs – jolt, jolt, jolt, with Mandy's eyes wincing slightly at every step.

The sun is out, briefly. Claire races ahead, whilst Mandy bowls along in her pushchair passively, not even babbling to herself as she does at home. The world moves past her: the blank walls of the 'backs', where the washing jigs around on the short lines; the wide empty road, lined by small grey houses and promenaded by the odd stray dog; the front gardens where daffodils wave in the wind. 'Flowers, flowers, nice flowers,' shrieks Claire, thrusting her face into the pushchair, pointing . . . but Barbara pushes on, and the flowers are left behind.

The baker's shop window is full of fresh bread and the round, flat loaves called 'stotty cakes'. Whilst Barbara and Claire go inside, and then into the butcher's, the greengrocer's and the grocer's, in the same short row of modern shops, Mandy waits. Sometimes she looks idly into the window; usually she stares unsmiling at the women who pass, and nod, and wave at her: 'Howay, darling. . . .' She does not know them. She is slowly learning that when Barbara and Claire walk from one shop there will be something pleasant for her. Inside the sweet shop Claire's hoarse imprecations have grown in volume – not that Barbara would dare to cross her on this matter. From a glass case crammed with goodies they choose penny lollies, green sugary jellies, parma violets, and a strange sickle-shaped jelly in the form of a pair of false teeth. When they come out Claire is dipping into her paper bag. Mandy clutches her Milky Bar and chews at the white chocolate with difficulty, cooing her appreciation.

There is another block of shops five minutes' walk away, across a patch of green about which Barbara moans with the air of someone who is repeating a complaint that has lost its force through habit: 'They *could* have put some swings for the kids here. Whoever planned this estate must have been male – he didn't have any kids anyway.'

On the way, she meets an acquaintance from round the corner – a big, plump girl called Lynn, who wears a cotton kerchief tied gypsy style, whose little girl trails behind her, crying.

Lynn explains: 'I've just given her a good hiding. She was crying for her daddy, so I said, I'll give you to your frigging daddy, and pack me bags, and let him get on with it.' Both women throw back their heads and laugh. Lynn adds that she is having 'an ornament party' that afternoon, and would Barbara like to come? She accepts before wheeling the pushchair on its way.

The sun has disappeared and Barbara hurries in from the wind. Bump, bump, bump backwards up the two flights of stone stairs, off with the coats and bonnets, more coal on the fire – and soon Mandy is being fed bread mashed into tomato soup, still sitting in her pushchair. Her mouth opens mechanically, but her eyes are closing; she rubs her face, crumpling suddenly like a rag doll. Barbara looks at the round, slack face: 'She's tired. I'll have to put her to bed.'

Now she has a dilemma. Outside it is bitterly cold – all attempts by the sun to play at spring have ceased. At 1 p.m. Claire must leave for her daily nursery session at the Bishop Harland Church of England Primary school. Mandy is tired, so Barbara does not want to get her wrapped up once more to face the cold walk. Aware that some people might frown on what she is doing, she puts the child in the cot in her bedroom, places the guard in front of the fire, washes Claire, and leaves for the school. She says she does not like leaving Mandy alone, but what harm can possibly come to her? Claire rushes down the stairs, keen as always to reach the modern school with its bright, spacious nursery department – pictures, blocks, tables and chairs, toys, books, a wooden slide. She loves it, and hardly pauses to kiss her mother before running in her slippers into the large room.

Mandy dozes off, wrapped warmly in her blankets.

On the way home Barbara decides to drop into the ornament party, because she promised she would. 'I can't stay,' she announces to a small room containing eight women, one man, six children and five packing cases full of newspaper-wrapped objects: 'I've left the bairn asleep.'

The women smoke and look fascinated as a tough-looking, well-dressed young woman with a broad Sunderland accent unwraps the objects one by one and arranges them on every possible surface. The suppliers of these ornaments pay her commission on what she sells; for offering the use of her house Lynn receives a free gift. Soon the room is filled with a variety of vases, boxes, wooden wall decorations, pottery animals and other useless and not very pretty objects. The young woman starts her patter: ' . . . You've got the glass rooster at £2.75, and next to it the small glass clown £3.65, and the medium glass clown at £4.99; there's your travelling polish set in a wallet if you know anyone that's going on a journey, £2.50 that is. Then you've got the green glass vase that also comes in aqua, looks lovely in aqua — that's £5.50. Here's the carved wooden boxes to put your bits in — the big one is £3.00 and the small one is £1.80. And there you've got the stone jam-jar for them that's too posh to keep it in the jar — £1.99 — I haven't got the money to buy the jam, never mind the jar. . . .' And so on. Each woman has been given a piece of paper and a pencil; Barbara neatly writes 'stone jam-jar' on hers.

She remembers Mandy and, ignoring the waiting sandwiches and cakes which turn the buying into a social occasion, she leaves. 'I think that they probably pay more for them getting them that way. You'd get them cheaper in Woollie's. I only ordered that jam-jar because I felt I had to buy something — and it was the cheapest, wasn't it?'

Mandy is asleep. The flat is silent. Usually Barbara spends her afternoons reading romantic novels from the library, enjoying the peace whilst Claire is at school.

'I was married two and a half years before I fell for Claire, and I didn't really like it. I was working full time in a butcher's in town, and I used to think if I had a little girl or boy at home it would be something to look forward to coming home for. I mean, what's life for? Marriage means bringing up your own children, looking after them, doing the best you can for them. Oh, I like having kids around — but I don't like *having* them.

'I really didn't look forward to having Mandy — being the second I suppose she's not a novelty. And I was more frightened about it because I knew what to expect after having Claire. It's mainly the pains — because I'm one of those people that can't relax. Even with gas and air, it doesn't help. But in the end it wasn't so bad. It was four and a half hours, and, compared with nineteen hours, it was very different. Mind, I worried all through that pregnancy. With Claire I didn't because I didn't know much about it. But with Mandy — I mean, I packed in smoking for four months, and then I started again, and I thought, 'What if there's something wrong with the baby?' I didn't take extra care of myself — I ate the same as I do now. But I always went to the clinic and the doctors. . . . I was very pleased with myself after I'd had her. She was seven pounds, fifteen ounces.

'Ray wasn't as excited as he was when I was having Claire, but he changed once I'd got her home. We got the ambulance home, and they were waiting for me when I got in, and the first words Claire said were, Oh, lovely baby. I'll never forget that. And she came straight away to put her arms around her. She was two years, nine months then. I'll never forget that.

'I've had problems with both of them. Claire's slow at her talking, and there's this problem with Mandy's bones. I'd been taking her to the welfare once a month, and each time the doctor would try to sit her up, and she wouldn't. Well, I was getting rather worried about it, and on this particular day she sat her up and examined her spine, and shook her head. I thought, Oh, Christ, there's something wrong with her. A couple of days later I got a card to take her to the specialist. I took her and he said they'd have to take her into hospital for tests. She had her first birthday on the Monday and went in on the Tuesday. She was in for a fortnight. They found out that her bones were still very soft and that it would be a long time before she got on her feet. So she has this calcium medicine every morning – Ray gives it to her in her bottle. And she's sitting up lovely now, and she's got her little boots to strengthen her ankles, and she's doing fine. They're very pleased.

'One thing that happened then – I was at the doctors, and he had this letter on his desk that had been written by the specialist to him, about Mandy. He left it open on top, and I was curious. I wanted to see what they said – 'cos they never tell you. But I wish I'd never looked now. It said that Mandy was a happy little girl and was coming along fine. It was about how good and happy she was. But there was just that one sentence. It said that the family life – or home life – leaves much to be desired. I didn't know who could have told him such a thing. It must have been the health visitor. But she never looked round the house. Mind you, a couple of times she's caught me unawares, she's come early and I haven't got my work done. She's only been once since I saw that. Well, I was upset, because there's no foundation for that kind of remark. I mean, I love the bairns, and they are well looked after. Well, to the best of my ability, shall I say? I told me mum, and she went up the wall. Ray said forget about it. And I thought – to hell. Why the bloody hell should I worry?'

From the bedroom there is a sound of gentle babbling – a private, thoughtful language full of contentment. It rises and falls as Mandy fingers each toe in turn and turns her head to gaze at the bars of her cot, with no urgency, rather with an acceptance that they are there. Barbara lifts her out and, taking her into the living room, allows a rare moment of closeness. The thin, pale woman, with the plump child on her knee, next to the glowing coals: 'Come on, fatso, give mummy a kiss. There! Howay, Mandy, howay, darlin', give us a kiss. . . .' Mandy makes mummy sounds, and gently fingers her face.

Then the slowly laced boots, bonnet, coat; the bumping down-stairs; the brisk walk to the school; and the wait outside whilst Barbara goes in for Claire. She is surrounded by noise: competitive girls playing netball, passing cars, the chatter of loitering mothers, the shrieks of the four-year-olds who rush out clutching plastic bags containing sticky jam tarts they have made, refusing to put their coats on, demanding sweets, fighting, laughing, provoking their mothers into furious cries: 'Claire, I *told you* to wait – *Claire*, man, *Clairrre!*' Slaps and shouts. Heads are thrust at her, hands wave in her face showing her things that move away before she can focus, voices shout in her ear – and loudest of all that of Claire. Mandy's brow is furrowed. Every day it is the same, this ritual – the same houses, the same noises, the same faces, fixing their pattern in her mind forever.

Back at home Barbara prepares the tea – scraping new potatoes, slicing carrots, shoving a tiny piece of pork in the oven to roast. Ray arrives home at about four-thirty and likes his tea promptly at five. Barbara believes in one good meal a day – on another evening it was braised liver, turnips and peas, though sometimes she does not eat any herself, existing a whole day on bread and butter, and cigarettes, because she is not hungry.

Whilst she is cooking the television is on, with Mandy in her pushchair by the side of it, and Claire rampaging around in front – picking up a toy, putting it down, watching the programme, rush-ing off, asking for a drink, running over to Mandy to hug her violently, squatting on the floor to watch the screen once more. And all the time Mandy watches her.

When Ray comes through the door the noise increases, ignored by Barbara who stays within her tiny kitchen, with its old-fashioned sink, old cooker, fridge, washing machine and not much else. Mandy sees her father pick up Claire and furiously holds out her arms to him. She sees him give Claire a round object, enticingly wrapped in gold and red foil, and feels the more frustrated, clutch-ing at the air. At last, satisfaction: she is lifted up, and can smell the mixture of skin and workclothes that she already associates so clearly and lovingly with the time of day. She laughs and strokes his ginger moustache, expecting – and receiving – her own chocolate treat. She does not notice her wet nappy – although he does, wiping his hand with an expression of mock disgust.

Finally Ray escapes to change into his clean jeans, then sits down for his tea. Barbara slides a laden plate in front of him, and his enormous mug of tea, then goes to feed Mandy a mashed mix of meat, potatoes and carrots. She says she does not want any herself. Claire, her mouth smeared with chocolate, picks at the food. The television brings news of the spring budget, and through the complexities of tax, Barbara and Ray listen for something that will affect them. 'Family allowance is going up,' cries Barbara, with surprise more than pleasure, 'that'll mean. . . .' She starts her rapid calculations.

At 5.45 Barbara leaves for work. Five nights a week she works in a bingo hall, for 45p an hour, from 6.30 until 10.30 p.m. With the extra 12p a night for 'calling the numbers', she brings home £9.62 a week, which pays the rent. Her reasons for working are not just economic; after a day in the flat with the children, and each day the same, she enjoys the escape to the boredom of the bingo hall, where at least she can chat to the other women. But this week she hates the thought of going. Each night it seems colder; outside there are already flurries of snow.

After she has gone Ray endures the couple of hours before he can put both girls in bed and indulge his addiction: television. Mandy first – that is easy, she makes no protest. Then Claire – who screams and fights and cries and stamps her feet at him, leaving her room four times after he has put her in bed, throwing herself against the living-room door like a tiny tornado. Then – silence, broken only by the occasional mutter from Claire and coo from Mandy, easily discernible through the paper-thin walls. He makes more tea, and lights a cigarette with relief.

'One reason that I'm not keen on Barbara working is that I'm here with them, and I tend to give in to them just to keep them quiet . . . . I've always liked kids, and as soon as I got married I wanted some bairns. They help a marriage, I think. Keep it together. Give you something you're both interested in. When I knew Babs was pregnant I was chuffed. And when Claire was born! The hospital was about a mile away, and I can't remember getting from there up to me mother's, and when I got there I couldn't get it out me mouth. It was all jumbled up; but they listened to the jibber-jabber, and thought, She must have had the baby. And I wanted a girl, and she *was* a girl. I wanted Mandy to be a girl, too – I said I didn't want no boys.

'I think it's because . . . I don't admit this much, but if you had a boy, and he grew up, instead of the family coming to you for decisions and help in the house, they might go to him. It would take some of your responsibility away. When you've lasses the responsibility is always yours – you're always their dad. But I suppose, now we've got the two girls, when we have another one in a couple of years, I won't mind if it turns out to be a boy.

'Claire was the first grandchild on her side and mine, and all the grandparents spoiled her. When she was younger and cried, we used to go in and get her out of the cot, instead of just leaving her, or settling her and coming out. We used to bring her in the front room, and she grew to expect it, like, and that's how she got spoilt. I wish I hadn't now. If I knew then what I know now it could have been different. But we didn't know a thing. You learn by your mistakes. There's a lot of things we did with Claire we won't do with Mandy. . . .

'I think you're more likely to spoil a girl as well. Take clothes — there's so many nice clothes you can buy them. You see a nice coat and think, She'd look nice in that, so when you've got a few coppers you go and buy it. But with a boy — a pair of jeans and a sweater and that's it. And toys — well, on the television now there's a doll advertised and it walks and talks and does all stupid things, and it costs about eight pounds, and I'd like to get her one of them. I was going to buy her a train set, but the wife wouldn't let me — she said that's for boys. It was mainly for me!

'They're good bairns. We wouldn't be without them, well — sometimes we would, but not really! I think part of the reason they're the way they are, or Claire, anyway, is that I'm not with them a lot. I look after them when she goes to work. And I work part of the weekend. So I feel guilty if I go off for a couple of pints Saturday or Sunday dinner time. I feel guilty about other things too. Like Claire talking. I feel as if, if I'd sat down with her more, and looked at books with her, then maybe she'd be talking. Mind you, the doctor said it's not our fault, she's just lazy . . . but I don't know. Now Mandy, she's picking up words very quickly. But Claire — she falls back on her double dutch. You can't understand a word she's saying. I feel more confident with Mandy, in a way.

'Yes, Babs saw this letter from the specialist to our doctor and it said that Mandy's home life left much to be desired. And I'd just done this place out! I thought, my decorating's not *that* bad, like. We always tidied up when she came — so I don't know how she could have arrived at that opinion. She was very snooty, like — the health visitor. You know, like one of those people that change once they get into a uniform.

'They tell you how to bring your children up — how can I put it? You shouldn't do this, you shouldn't do that. But that sounds as if all bairns are the same, and they're not. All bairns are different.

They've all got their own personalities. And the social services – I've got no regard for them at all. It upsets me to hear of these cases of child battering, and the social services have given the bairns back to the parents! They shouldn't. But *they* are the homes that leave a lot to be desired, not ours.

'I went down to the housing office at the civic centre to ask if we could have a transfer, and they make you feel that small – you know, you're in your work clothes, like. They said there was no chance. I'd like a house. For the sake of a garden, like. I mean, us: we eat in this room, we watch television in this room, the bairns have to play in this room. There isn't room to swing a cat. There's only room for one person in the kitchen, really. It would be nice to have a kitchen looking out on a garden, with plenty of room for the washing machine – and the bairns could run straight out.

'It sounds as if it's something that I've read in a book, but it isn't – I mean, that children like to express themselves. They like to go out and pretend they're animals, and take all their dolls out, and that. Now I bought Claire a Wendy house, but there's nowhere to put it. I've managed to put it up in her bedroom, but she can't get inside it – the room's too small. Now if we had a garden she could have it out there, and go out there on her own, and pretend she was talking to fairies in it, and then she could come back in and – like – tell us what they said. But here, she's playing right in front of us, and we're shouting at her to be quiet because of the people downstairs, so there's nothing to talk about, if you know what I mean. Bairns need to be able to play out. Make up their own games. Be themselves. I like them to believe in fairies and Santa Claus and things like that – fantasies are important. I tell them at Christmas Santa Claus is coming. But then, in a flat this size there's nowhere to hide the presents. Mandy sleeps in our room, and Claire ran in and saw me putting them on top of the wardrobe. It spoils it.'

Voices from television give a detailed breakdown on the budget.

Ray says that he earns £1.11 an hour, plus bonus. 'We manage, just about. Her money pays the rent, and I give her between £30 and £35 a week for her wages. I'd like to be able to buy the bairns something nice – I mean walk in and get it. By the time I've saved up, it's gone up a pound. I think a married man with two children should have at least £65 a week to live on. When I see old Healey standing up there I think, I'll believe him when I see something in my wage packet. It's funny – politics. I don't think they really care about you – not the individual. I think they think in mass. The system's like that; obviously you can't be an individual. But you feel, like if there's an increase, it's good because everybody's getting it, but *you're* not someone special. Hard to explain it, really. I suppose it's vanity, like. I think everybody likes to feel they're somebody special, everybody does. Like if you've got somebody at home, waiting for you, you're somebody special to them. Like your kids. I feel when I come in — *I'm* their dad. If some people don't have that it must make them feel a bit lost, a bit adrift. I felt like that before I was married.'

One morning Barbara took her children to the Hylton Castle Health Centre — a long walk in the cold wind. The low building was new and pleasing, with an airy waiting room. Mandy was dumped in the scales, smiling and cooing and not wanting to get out. The motherly attendant converted from the kilos to twenty-seven pounds. They went through to the doctor's room, where a large, bespectacled Scottish woman sat writing the notes of a previous child. She welcomed them warmly. 'Och, sit down Mrs Green, and how's the little ones? How's Mandy?'

Mandy sat on her mother's lap, fascinated by the rattles, the tiny buttons she had to pick up, the coloured bricks — all devices to test her responses. 'Good, good,' exclaimed the doctor, when she accomplished each task with ease. 'Now, can you just take her nappy off, Mrs Green?'

Strange hands, prodding, touching, squeezing her knees, turning her over, holding her up — her fat little legs refused to bear her weight. Mandy did not protest — her expression showed amazement. She was quickly dressed again — and all through the doctor did not halt her noises of approval.

'The baby's coming along *fine*.'

'Yes, ever since she was in hospital. It's made all the difference. She has her Calciferol every morning.'

'Yes, Mrs Green, she'll soon be walking.'

Then it was Claire's turn. The child stood by the doctor with her trusting little grin, looking up at the motherly woman who seemed to be giving too much attention to Mandy. She wanted so much to please. The doctor tested her vocabulary with a picture book, but although she could recognize 'bus', 'ball' and 'cat', she could not talk about them. 'What worries you, Mrs Green?'

'Well, I think she ought to be talking better — in sentences.'

'Well, I'll see her when she gets to school, and we'll have her seen

by the child psychologist. He'll test her. But she's a great girl —
they're both great girls, Mrs Green.'

Barbara told her about the neighbours below them who had been
complaining about the noise. The doctor tutted sympathetically.

'Have you told the health visitor about this?'

'I did, but. . . .'

'Have you tried the social services?'

'I thought about that.'

'Yes, you try them, Mrs Green. Tell them your bairns need to run
around and can't, and that the little one has a bad chest and needs
more fresh air, and say your nerves are shattered. You have to lay it
on with a trowel.'

Barbara seemed glad of this chance to talk.

'Bairns living in flats go right back. They're being held back.
Sometimes, Doctor, I feel sorry for Claire, when I'm shouting at her
for making so much noise because I'm worried about them downstairs. And she can't talk to me, so she shouts too. And Mandy's just
sitting there watching, and as soon as she starts walking it will be
twice as bad.'

The gas fire hissed slightly. The doctor made reassuring and
soothing sounds, repeating her advice, saying it would be 'sorted
out'.

Outside, Barbara puzzled slightly on the implications of her
advice. 'I don't know how to set about doing that — I mean, seeing
the social services. Do you phone them up? Do you go down to the
civic centre? I suppose I could tell the health visitor, but I don't
know her name. . . .' She shook her head: 'I don't know, you worry
about having them, and you worry about bringing them up.'

When they had arrived home after the windy walk, when the
children were playing as usual on the floor, and Mandy was screaming because Claire had taken an old torn book from her, the telephone rang. It was Ray.

'Yes,' Barbara told him, 'Mandy's twenty seven pounds, and
Claire is thirty six pounds. . . . What do you mean? She's putting it
on. She says they're coming on lovely. . . .'

He came home as usual, dispensing the sweets, commenting that
there was no clean nightie for Claire, and wanting to hear once more
what the doctor had said. The visit to the welfare was a major event.
After tea he got ready to go out to the Redhouse Workingmen's
Club.

He sat with his father, drinking a pint of beer, whilst most of the
eyes were down for a game of bingo. The atmosphere was warm,

friendly, the large room slightly shabby with use, not neglect. Ray Green said: 'What I'd really like my bairns to do is make something of themselves. Not like me. I was going to follow my dad and be a decorator, but the bottom fell out of that with all this do-it-yourself. Then I was going to be a butcher, but the bloke I was sort of apprenticed to died, and if he hadn't I'd have stopped in the business, and I'd have been a butcher by now. Whereas now, they say where are you? And I say . . . er . . . I'm a roadsweeper. You've got a brush and you're picking things up, and people think you're daft sometimes.

'I left school when I was fifteen, but if *they* wanted to go to college or something I wouldn't stop them. Not unless they're as thick as me. They'll get nowhere then. Barbara doesn't care, like, she says they'll make up their own minds. But me . . . What I say about Mandy is this: she'll be a canny lass when she's got over this bother with her bones, and I'd like her to make something of herself so that people come to *her*. Do you understand my meaning? I don't want her to have to crawl to anyone for anything. I want them to come to her. Until she gets married, like. Then I do think a woman's place is in the home. . . .

'Oh, you can't worry too much about your bairns. Some bairns are brats – I suppose *mine* are brats! But they're great. If owt happened to them I'd be under a bus, me. I'd have nothing left to live for. There's the bairns to come home to – that's why I rush for the early bus, just to see them.'

3 Gemma

It was Maria Montessori, the Italian educationist, who wrote:

The liberty of the child should have as its limit the collective interest; as its form, what we universally consider good breeding. We must therefore check in the child whatever offends or annoys others, or whatever tends towards rough or illbred acts.

Gemma's mother would certainly agree with that. Yet at the beginning of the twentieth century Montessori was a revolutionary, whose philosophy or 'system' was built around the needs of the individual child – and the necessity of achieving a balance between freedom and responsibility, creativity and order. Her prose reflects the tension, switching from the tersest, most conventional expressions to the kind of idealistic, child-centred sentiments Gemma's teachers would find sympathetic. She wrote:

We cannot know the consequences of suffocating a spontaneous action at the time when a child is just beginning to be active; perhaps we suffocate life itself. Humanity shows itself in all its intellectual splendour during this tender age as the sun shows itself at the dawn, and the flower in the first unfolding of its petals; and we must respect religiously, reverently, these first indications of individuality.

That was in 1912.

Sixty-six years later, Gemma Wood, innocent channel, like her friends, for all these ideas and more, crouches in the Montessori room at the Jabberwocky Nursery School in Bath, carefully doing a puzzle. She plays on a small green mat – the Montessori idea of a defined work space of the child's own, for which she is responsible. The room is light and bright, its Georgian proportions intact, with low blue-painted shelves along one wall, on which wooden equipment (geometric shapes which slot into trays, boxes and rods of varying lengths) is arranged – the Montessori idea that children could best learn from simple pleasing equipment which would teach them shape and form. There is a piano; an enormous black and white Chinese drawing of sunflowers dominates the room.

Gemma is three, with a round face and cropped fair hair. Her expression is habitually composed. Follow her around the room, see with her a tray containing little baskets of dried pulses – the orange of the lentils contrasting with the smooth white of haricots; a box of exactly fitting wooden blocks in different colours; a pile of puzzles jigsawed from coloured wood. What to choose? Nothing here. So through to the library, the quiet room where the children can start to read by matching lettercards against the coloured alphabet frieze that runs round the room. Stand watching the children playing with books ... wonder whether to stop ... then escape, through the dark passage-room where boys fight and shout, through to the spacious studio. Look up with Gemma: the ceiling is high and white with a centre skylight, the walls are snowy brick, the floor red tiles. Chinese kites twirl in the space between ceiling and floor; plants, fish, gerbils, easels with splodgy paintings, tables of clay and Play-Doh fill each corner of the huge room with live activity. What to do? The question is asked twenty times a morning. And Gemma thinks and chooses, perhaps returning to the Montessori room to wander round again, always looking, until at last something attracts, something to absorb, her own choice, on her own small mat.

It costs Gemma's parents £48 a term to send her to Jabberwocky – though on Mondays she stays home with her mother. Home is a modern, four-bedroom house, on a new estate built in the grounds of an old country house on the edge of Bath. The land is steep and terraced: the Woods' rear garden ascends to the level of the upstairs windows. Their road is equally steep; a cul-de-sac of pleasant houses, with two garages each and well-kept gardens studded with daffodils and tulips. Rowena Wood dislikes the reconstituted Bath stone the houses are built from, which tries hard to be authentic and fails dismally – flat yellow instead of mellow gold.

When Rowena and Bob Wood (who are both thirty two) first moved to Bath, she was working as a qualified quantity surveyor and actually completed some work for that site. Then she became pregnant with Benjamin, who is now six, worked at home for a while, then gave up when Gemma was born. Now she reads proofs for a publishing company, gardens enthusiastically, bakes delicious bread, and involves herself with meetings of the National Organization of Women and a fringe organization of the Bath Festival. Bob Wood is a successful and energetic executive with a progressive American company called Herman Miller which produces modern furniture from a new, well-designed factory in the centre of Bath. He enjoys his work, aware at the same time that success brings with it more responsibility and less time to spend with his family. But

Gemma sits and watches television on a leather and chrome Charles Eames chair, surrounded by modern furniture produced by her father's firm, knowing that though her father may go away on the occasional business trip, mother is always there.

Rowena Wood: 'I couldn't possibly have worked once I had Gemma because I was too tired. It was a terribly basic existence from day to day – to live through the fact that you'd have completely interrupted nights, that you were tired when you woke up, and that as soon as you'd had breakfast she'd be screaming again. I don't know why she was like that.... She was a frustrated baby. She didn't become better until she spoke, and once she could speak she could maybe express some of this pent-up feeling. I think she didn't want to be a little baby, she wanted to be grown, she wanted to be the *child*. If she had been born in China she would have been carried everywhere on her mother's back, seeing things. Always she would stop crying when I was carrying her – the closeness – she was fine then. But had I had Gemma first it would have put me off. Having had Benjamin, an easy baby, I did realize they weren't all like that. The fact that one had had a good one – one thought, Well, it can't be me.

'On some occasions it all became too much, but you see, she was always ... I mean, when she was good she really was very good, and when she was bad she was horrid! She could be the most lovely child, she had these big enormous eyes – and Benjamin was at a lovely age, very nice and bright. So I never in fact got absolutely desperate. I never got to the stage of shaking her. I somehow managed to cope. I don't know why. It was probably an easy case for baby battering, you know, with that noise going on; and I have an absolutely tremendous sympathy for any mother who batters a child, because I could so understand it.

'Had we had Gemma in a one-bedroom ghastly flat with no garden, and all the other social pressures bearing in on us ... well, if you had this baby, and couldn't sleep at night, the neighbours complaining.... We were terribly lucky. Our neighbour was a friend. She understood that the terrible noise was only Gemma. But you could have a family who would get nasty about it. If you had that kind of pressure on you I can understand that you could really turn on the child because the child was causing it all. I never felt like that, even though there were odd moments I wished I'd never had her! I think you were aware it *could* happen and you controlled yourself. And she was so pathetic, I suppose....

'I don't think one ever really regrets that you've had them. I've often thought if one had a deformed child or something . . . but you speak to people about it and they say it never makes any difference. They still love them. I feel that maybe *because* Gemma was such a problem as a baby it gave one quite a maternal feeling, because she was so dependent on *me*. She'd have nothing really to do with Bob. It had to be me. It was a very close relationship and I think that's probably why I feel very close to her still. It was very much the two of us. She wouldn't be placated by anyone else. It had to be me.'

Every evening, after the bath she shares with Benjamin in their own bathroom, Gemma goes to the airing cupboard to choose her clothes for the next day. Rowena's smooth ironing is piled in little heaps; Gemma knows her own pile and deliberates: the blue jumper? Or the white one? Certainly the red trousers. It is her ritual. She will not wear the clothes she has worn the day before, even if they are still clean; and she will resolutely go down to breakfast in her pyjamas rather than wear those clothes, should Rowena (for practical reasons) suggest such an alteration to the pattern.

Gemma dresses herself carefully, even though she is only three, making sure that nothing is inside out, that the label is at the back; even that things match. She likes to be in control.

On Mondays she and Rowena might drive over to the allotment on the slopes of Lansdowne Hill. With views of Bath around her, surrounded by the well-kept plots in which the local Italian families grow garlic and artichokes (the British concentrate on carrots and beans), Gemma will splash about in her wellingtons watching her mother pull pale fat leeks from the damp soil, observing a worm, or digging with a stick in one corner of the allotment, calling it her own. There may be seedlings to be transferred from the boxes that litter Rowena's windowsills, or soil to be turned. Gemma loves going there – a tiny carbon of the woman who digs in jeans and boots, with short neat hair.

On Tuesdays, Wednesdays, Thursdays and Fridays Gemma goes to her school, Rowena alternating with Liz, mother of Gemma's best friend Dan Hall, in fetching and carrying up and down the steep hills of Bath. So Gemma travels in her mother's rusty estate (Bob drives a new Rover, a company car) or in Liz's tiny Fiat which strains on slopes, and always chatters with Dan in the back as if they were mutually attracted adults meeting for the first time. 'I've got my red trousers on, look. My mummy's taking me to Sainsbury's this afternoon. . . . When we get to school I'm going to do a painting, what are you going to do – you can do one with me.' Dan Hall generally agrees with what she says.

Jabberwocky School takes up the ground floor of a classically beautiful house in Lansdowne Crescent, which was bought by an American five years ago. He decided to start a private nursery school run on Montessori lines, and after some initial difficulties, the school established itself. Now Lesley Flash, a qualified nursery teacher, runs the school on £5000 a year, with the help of two other qualified staff and two or three unpaid helpers. Periodically the stream of children – all of thirty at the most – entering and leaving the school incenses the inhabitants of the crescent so much that they are moved to get up a petition opposing the school's existence, proposals to increase the numbers or open in the afternoon, or whatever.

Lesley Flash believes that at the root of their protests is a conviction that children somehow lower the tone of one of Bath's most celebrated landmarks. 'Children raise their voices, and move their arms and legs, and a lot of people find the idea of them a disturbance. It is small-town politics of the most conservative sort.'

Gemma and Dan run into the controversial school, changing into their slippers in the hall. Into the studio, to one of the low shelves – and they take glue, paper, and a tray of seeds, milk bottle tops and pasta, immediately starting work. Glue is squeezed on to the paper, and then the different materials are sprinkled on top; what does not stick is shaken away. They ask for nothing; they complete their pictures – milky-way straggles of brown seeds, beige grain and orange lentils, spiked by yellow macaroni and wood shavings – and place them carefully on another shelf to dry. Gemma wants to start another 'sticky', as she calls it, but Dan has the glue. Impatient, she watches: 'Dan, you've had it for a long, long time, Dan, you've had the glue for *too* long. . . .' Until at last she gives it up and runs out of the room, leaving him with his tongue out, laboriously sticking.

In the Montessori room Gemma does not hesitate. She walks to the box where the mats are kept, takes one, unrolls it, then picks a wooden puzzle from a shelf, tipping the pieces out on to her tray: two red deer and a yellow rabbit in a landscape. The puzzle is unusually difficult because the pieces are coloured both sides, reversing the shapes into a maze of possibilities. Gemma tries for ten minutes, in complete silence, except to mutter to herself: 'Does that one go there?' She expects no answer, her mind is only concerned with its own problem: 'It's a very *funny* puzzle.'

Finally, with an expression of resignation, she gives up and replaces the jumbled pieces of puzzle upon the shelf, choosing another. The following day she will go straight to the difficult one again, this time asking, 'Show me how to do it – 'cos then I can do it myself.'

Now she tips out a simple puzzle of animals, and completes it in a few minutes – not looking up to ask for praise, but simply replacing it upon the shelf, a look of self-contained satisfaction. Gemma needs no one, not even Dan, who runs up to ask hopefully, 'Did you look for me, Gemma?'

She does not reply, but when he copies her and takes his own puzzle from the shelf, she asks, 'Do you want me to open the box for you?' and when the pieces are displayed, she adds, 'That's a very *little* puzzle. That's a very *easy* puzzle, Dan. Do you want me to help you with it?' He does.

A child rings a bell loudly in the room. 'Time to clear up, Dan – it's circle time.' This is the one time in the morning when all the children come together, to form a circle in the Montessori room. The teachers and helpers take turns to 'take' the circle each day.

Today it is the turn of Bruce, a shambling young American boy with long hair and a beard, whose tendency is laconically to ask the children to do things, then look vaguely surprised when they do not. He is helping at the school for one year, before returning to the States to 'do a course'. First he takes the register, calling Harriet, Helen, Gemma, Matthew, Hugh, James, Gabriel, Leda, Celestine, and noting their replies of 'Here I am!' – Gemma's the promptest, the clearest.

'Now, what shall we all talk about? Today is a good spring day, I've noticed all the flowers are out. What else happens in spring-time?'

Silence. Then a boy replies, 'Sometimes a fair comes.'

'That's a good one. What do the flowers do?'

'They grow.'

'What do the farmers do in the springtime?'

'They plant corn.'

'And bluebells come out. . . .'

The children are sitting attentively, though Bruce's manner is soporific.

'Er . . . what else can you tell me about spring?'

Gemma takes her thumb from her mouth: 'It's not cold.'

Break time – which means that the children go when they want to the small table in the studio, where Lesley has already placed a plate of roughly cut wholemeal bread, a carton of margarine, and a dish of raw carrots cut into sticks. There is a jug of milk and a selection of mugs, so that the children can help themselves, learning to butter their own bread and share what is there. One day Lesley will make scones with one or two of the children, so that they are ready by break, hot from the small oven, and the margarine melts all over them, running down small fingers, being licked ... and causing the children to squabble slightly about who has or has not had a precious half.

Gemma's role is that of organizer – she will sit at the table and tell the naughtiest boys in the class that they mustn't, they really mustn't do whatever it is they are doing – like push, or grab, or spill. Dan Hall follows her, mopping up some spilt milk without being asked, trotting around with his usual expression of gentle eagerness. In the background, the gentle strains of a Mozart piano concerto fill the room.

Lesley Flash: 'When Gemma first came to the school she was two and a half and cried a lot. Perhaps she started too young. She didn't want to let her mother go. Now it is noticeable that she does not want to form relationships with any of us adults. Sometimes she wants your attention – but then she wants it all or none. You sense that her mother comes first. So at school she keeps herself to herself, but gets on methodically with her work. Her friendship with Dan Hall is important, though. . . . In their case the fact of their friendship rather determines what they get from school. Sometimes I will split them up. In Gemma's case the fact that she has got Dan means that she has even less need for us. She overshadows him a bit, but he is such a lovely boy it doesn't matter.

'You can tell very little about the homes the children at this school come from. They're very mixed. Except that you could say that the 'hippy' children are more disruptive. And you get the stunted children of some middle-class families who have no initiative – girly girls, and boys who are wet. It's easier to make relationships with them when you don't know the parents. Then you don't get involved with the parents' expectations. My biggest problem is parents! Because this is called a school they bring to it all their expectations of a school. Now, I think that nursery school gives children a head start, but not in terms of attainment, which is what the parents want. I think it gives them confidence – and they're far, far cleverer than we give them credit for. When they get to proper school, all that is knocked out of them – the lack of stimulus, the time spent on organization rather than on doing. I find it depressing to think of them going on to that. . . . That's why I teach nursery school.'

Gemma is back with her puzzles. Some days she will spend as long as fifteen minutes completing one, methodical in all her actions. An easy one is returned to the shelf the minute it is finished, with a look of near-irritation that it did not present more of a challenge, another easy one rejected, a hard one picked – and a friendly little girl who offers to help her summarily rejected. Gemma sits down on a brown mat to start her puzzle when Dan comes running in to tell her that nobody is using the easel, so they both can paint. 'Oh dear, oh dear,' tuts Gemma, but starts to put the pieces back into the box. 'Wait for me, Dan, wait there,' she calls – but he has gone. For a fraction of a second she looks tempted to follow; instead she repeats her refrain, 'Oh dear, oh dear,' completing her clearing with perfect discipline before following him into the studio.

Dan has already donned an apron and is squeezing his own paint into pots from large plastic containers. He is eager, measuring the yellow, green, blue and red, choosing a brush. The preparation takes a long time, with Gemma frowning when she discovers that she has forgotten one colour from the range: 'Something's missing. . . . Yellow! Oh dear, let's have yellow.'

Two of the boys have asked for rock music, so the strains of Mozart have given way to a rollicking record called 'Top of the Tots'. Gemma paints a thick white square. Then she fills in half the centre with red, and the other half with yellow. Stands back to look. A piece of abstraction . . . but to her horror the thick paint begins to run from the edges of the white square in little rivulets to the bottom of the page, and the red and the yellow merge their boundaries. Messy. At once she loses interest, and mixes the red, yellow and white into a vast splodge. 'I'm painting orange.' Orange what? 'Just orange.'

On the other side of the easel, Dan has painted three rows of blue waves. In the centre is a yellow stripe, which turns into a green man, huge and square with red circular eyes.

'It's a man in the waves, and those are his glasses to stop the water getting into his eyes. When I was on my holidays my daddy lifted me up because a big wave came, and I was frightened.' He puts a broad strip of yellow at the bottom of the picture for the sand.

Gemma has splodged green on top of the orange. Slowly the original neat square turns brown, losing its form. 'They are colours,' she explains. But as she adds blue, then more yellow, then some red, the painting becomes muddier and muddier, and more indistinct.

Dan has painted a row of blue dots on his yellow sand. They are the footprints. White and pinkish grey blobs to one side of the waves are the seagulls flying down over the man – whose body is blue because it is under the water, whereas his head is not. On the horizon is the red square of a hotel, looming over the waves. Dan explains the details proudly, in the voice of a master: his mother designs clothes, his father paints.

Gemma is already washing up, leaving her painting behind. Dan takes his down, puts it to dry on a shelf, then stops by a table on which some sea shells are arranged, turning them over and over in his hands, carefully measuring their curves, studying the colours, the shades of his own seagulls.

The next day Gemma neglects Dan, and plays 'mummies and daddies' with a large quiet boy called Toby. They pretend to bake, then Gemma says to him, 'I'm mummy, and you can be the baby.'

A little girl called Vivien comes up to join in, undeterred by Gemma's 'You're not playing.'

Gemma and Vivien wrestle over a rolling pin and some Play-Doh, until a boy shouts from across the room, 'Stop grabbing, Gemma!'

Toby finally gets the picture and protests, 'No, I'll be the *daddy*.'

'It's not *your* playschool, Gemma,' mutters Vivien angrily, and retreats to her own table to make her own 'cake', whilst Gemma and Toby share a table by her side, not speaking to her.

At circle time, Toby will not leave her side. Whilst Lesley is asking the children to show what they have brought for the class to talk about, he sneaks an arm round Gemma's shoulders. She removes it. He attempts to put her arm around him. She becomes pink with embarrassment, twisting away, replacing her own arm by her side. But Toby will not give up. Four times he tries to put his arm around her, and four times she pulls away, scarlet with confusion. Lesley does not notice. Nobody notices when Toby actually tries to kiss Gemma Wood, and she turns to him with a dignified '*Stop* that', like the heroine of an old-fashioned romance.

Rowena Wood: 'Gemma will only go to Jabberwocky until the end of the summer term. In September she'll start at the Hermitage. It's a small private school for little girls. We decided to send Benjamin to the state school, St John's, because it is a good school, and we had the idea that we would switch him into the private sector at seven. But it's no good sending a child if he can't cope with it. You have to have a fairly bright child who will survive in that system – you can't send a child who is mediocre, because it's a hard-working situation, and Bob far more than me was very much aware that he didn't want Benjy to go into an academic situation he couldn't cope with. . . .'

Bob Wood: 'Rowena was really far more successful than me at school. She went to a grammar school, and got on very well, really. I went to public schools, and I really wasn't very good at all. It was a great problem . . . not knowing what I could be good at. It was very hard. But my parents were very understanding; they took me away from the conventional school and sent me to a Rudolph Steiner school. There all the emphasis is on the individual. One example, when I went there I suddenly learnt about painting. At the prep school it wasn't encouraged – I used to do these tiny neat little drawings – I wasn't good at it at all. But suddenly people were encouraging one to play with the paint, really use it.

'It was an important thing there – very exciting. And music. I was always quite good at that but had never been encouraged before, and now I was. I think that if you can give those things to your children, an understanding of painting and music and books, and things like that, then they will always have it to fall back on. You can't remove it from them. We may reach a situation where with more leisure they have to do those things. But that's not the reason. It's back to what I call values, though it is hard to put into words. More than anything I want Benjamin and Gemma to grow up with a strong sense of values, and I am talking in the broadest sense. You know – at one of the schools we went to see for Benjamin there was a little boy who had done well in his exam or something, and his parents had given him a briefcase. It was huge . . . you know? A *full-size* briefcase. It was almost as big as him.' He shakes his head, laughing. 'And I don't know. . . . You felt he had to grow to fit that briefcase: there was no other option for him. When I talk about values I mean that I want them to realize that there is more to being alive than . . . material things. It's a question of developing as a full individual, so that you can make your own decisions about what you want to do.'

Rowena: ' . . . So having made the decision that Benjamin was going to be educated privately, we had to send them both. What you do for one you have to do for both. And because you don't change little girls at seven, we had to start her in at the ground floor. I think that one wanted to develop in her the sort of manners and a nice approach to things which she will get at this school because the headmistress is a tremendous believer in discipline. They do nice things there. When you go into a classroom they stand up and say good morning to the teacher, and in the corridor they say, Excuse me, rather than just barge through ... and, just little things like that. I prefer her to grow up with that. She will have something of an assurance about her. That is what the private schools can give to girls especially – assurance, and the manners I think are important.

'I think Gemma is going to be quite clever generally. She's got this tremendous will; she just carries on. She'll know what she wants and she'll do it. Hopefully, if that's channelled correctly she'll be all right. I think we're going to have ghastly battles when she gets to the age of wanting to go out to discos – that will be difficult – but one hopes that one has set her up with the right kinds of values. I hope that she'll come back to home as a base.

'I don't particularly want her to turn out to be brilliantly clever at all, but I want her to have a broad sort of education. The school has such an influence – you don't know what they're doing. That is why we have chosen this school for Gemma. One is sure that she will come back from there echoing things that we have already said to her at home. In no way would I disagree with the argument that it is an elitist thing, that you're sending her in with children of similar background, from parents who want a good education for their children, small classes – and you are dependent on that parental background. I just think it would be hard for us if she came home from school, and not so much flouted our authority ... but was developing, you know, not very nice habits we wouldn't have instigated.

'I think it's especially important for a girl – she should be able to hold her own in any sort of company and feel at ease. I wouldn't say I am a great believer in this women's lib situation. To my mind it's been taken just too far – I'm sort of digressing a bit, but if it almost came to the stage where it decried the role of a woman and mother, I think it would be wrong. Because we may be getting the situation where girls are growing up and thinking it's not the thing to do. They want something which proves that '*I*' can do it as well as a man. I think that can cause them, in the long term, some degree of unhappiness. I mean I'd like Gemma ... I mean, I quite look forward to my grandchildren. I'd be disappointed if both of them married and had no children. I read somewhere that it's good when you're a mother because you see a generation, but when you're a grandmother you're head of a family which has gone on a generation more – which must be a nice sort of feeling. I think it's a tremendously complex subject but in a way it is a preservation feeling: that the human race will continue. It will be nice to have grandchildren because you can enjoy them as children without the responsibility, and it's very nice to share things as you get older – and you see this young brightness and innocence about life, and you can share something of it. . . . Because of that I wouldn't want Gemma to grow up particularly thinking she's got to fulfil herself as a woman or prove that she can do some superb job and hold her own completely.'

All week the replies had been coming back: brightly coloured scraps of card which announced that Dan and Toby and Tilly and Elizabeth and Alexander and the others could come to Gemma's birthday party. The party dominated the days. Gemma rode on the trolley at Sainsbury's whilst her mother bought crisps, sweets, jaffa cakes and chocolate for prizes, sliced bread for sandwiches – all for her party. Back at home she watched whilst Rowena laboriously and methodically checked the bill against the actual items, ticking them off in turn so as to be sure the cashier had not made a mistake.

Gemma rebuked Ben for pretending to steal the crisps – 'They're for my party,' she said. Ben, for his part, grew more difficult as the week went on – partially jealous, partially patronizing of his little sister who was so excited at the prospect of a party which would not be his.

One night they were sweeping the kitchen floor after cutting paper, when his continual teasing made Gemma cry. Rowena looked harassed, shouted at him, then smiled ruefully at the furious tear-streaked little girl who still continued her task. Ben grinned: 'Gemma's sweeping up all her tears. That's why she cried – to make the floor wet so she could clean it.' And then Rowena laughed.

All week Bob and Rowena had wondered what to buy Gemma for her birthday present. 'It sounds dreadful, doesn't it?' Rowena remarked, 'But I can't think of anything that she hasn't got.'

The Woods do not believe in giving valuable presents. Many of the children's toys are bought from the second-hand columns, although Bob Wood earns an extremely good salary. '*We* buy very little (though we have two super sets of grandparents who buy them super presents). I don't see the point. It would be very bad for them if they thought that everything appeared when they wanted it. Benjamin saw an old bike being made into a nice bike for him, and that's how it should be. I mean, I'm often amazed by people. I think middle-class people tend to spend less than the working class do. I wouldn't want to make that generalization, but I meet the people in Bob's factory, and the things they give their children! Expensive things. . . . The national poll I read on how much people spent on their children at Christmas staggered me – £20 to £30. Never in a month of Sundays would we spend that on the kids.'

In the end they decided on a scooter, because a child at Jabberwocky had brought a simple, well-designed wooden one to school. Rowena found it in Tridias toyshop, examined it, then asked Bob to go and look. He decided that the wood might rot, that the scooter was too expensive. So finally Rowena went to the Argos cash-and-carry and bought a bright red metal scooter.

The scooter delighted Gemma when she unwrapped it on the morning of 31st April. She and Ben had risen early and crept downstairs to find the presents. Outside it was cold, and rain dripped from the trees.

All day Rowena made the brown egg sandwiches, speared tiny sausages with sticks, and arranged the cakes and biscuits and potato rings on paper plates – whilst Gemma played with her scooter, desperate by 3 p.m. to change into her party dress. It was in long, flower-sprigged cotton with a pink velvet ribbon at the waist – and Gemma looked incongruous, a small determined boy-girl in feminine clothing.

At 3.30 the children start to arrive. The house seems strangely quiet, and Toby, Tilly, Alexander and the rest talk in whispers and some of them cling to their mothers. Each child carries a present which Gemma falls upon, throwing the cards aside, ripping off the paper: 'Not *another* pencil case! That makes two. . . . Now I've got *another* pencil.'

Rowena and her sister enthuse, 'Isn't that lovely, aren't you lucky?' as if wanting to cover up for the typical childish candour and covetousness. Bob Wood, kneeling on the floor in jeans and sweater as a change from the elegant suits he wears to his office, plays with Ben and the boys, occasionally pausing to turn over the record of nursery rhymes which pipes constantly in the background. The parents deposit their children and drive off, leaving the little ones to shuffle and suck their thumbs. School is different – there you have a reason to be together, but parties are adult inventions, and the children have no small talk to carry them through the silence. They look at each other, at the presents, at the other toys in the corner, unwilling to move until Rowena announces that the games will begin.

Musical bumps – and the children bounce nervously around longing for, yet dreading that moment of silence when they will have to act. And it is confusing – when Dan Hall is the first to be eliminated, he carries on playing – not yet understanding the real banishment of being 'out'.

Then it is the 'Farmer's in His Den', and when one or two of the children refuse to play, Rowena and her sister and another mother who has stayed join the ring, smiling with the self-conscious look of people caught out in their *own* ritual, in the rhymes and deeds they are passing on to the children. In the odd quietness, the nursery LP plonks out the familiar tunes: 'Old MacDonald', 'Ring O' Roses', and one called 'My Small Ring'. The children passively form their ring, with Gemma in the centre. The others walk around her, as she sings the invitation to join her small ring. A child joins her, and another, and another, the inner ring growing and growing, until at last all the children have passed to that second stage. . . .

Rowena: 'One romanticises things most horribly as years go on. And you remember. I mean, I remember Benjamin's fourth birthday with a lovely feeling: that everyone was happy and it was a sunny day. And I see that as Gemma gets bigger she'll no longer be able to snuggle on my lap – she won't be able to do all that. One can almost – not that one would want it, really – feel the need to perpetuate, to have little children around. But you have to call a halt! But you know, I'm really enjoying them growing up. It does give one quite a degree of pleasure to see them master things. When Benjamin could first ride a two-wheeler, when he could first write his name, and when he first started to read: it gave one a superb feeling.

'And Gemma is learning things. . . . The other day they were outside and they said, What's this flower? Because when there are wild flowers about I try to learn to identify them. It teaches them something – looking at things. I said I didn't know it, and he said, Let's look it up in the book – which I thought was very good. I thought, that's nice. I think that'll become more fun as they both grow older, when you do things together, and they take a more active role. They won't be taken by me and told. They'll come to me, and tell me.'

The children tire of games. Outside the rain has stopped, and Rowena promises that after tea they can all run outside and take the bikes and prams to play with in the steep garden. So they file through the dining room, with its white circular table and floor covered with toys, into the kitchen for tea.

The table is laid with red and white paper plates and mugs, the food arranged in the middle. First they grab the crisps, have to be persuaded to eat the egg sandwiches, and slurp their orange, always waiting for the cakes and biscuits. They munch in silence, whilst Bob takes flash photos with seriousness. Full with crisps and potato rings, they still grab the home-made brownies Rowena puts before them, and the other sweet goodies which replace the mangled sandwiches. The adults stand round, nibbling, pouring orange, and smiling at the strangeness of children who cannot talk to each other.

At last it is time for the cake. Rowena puts it right in front of Gemma: a crowd of jelly teddy bears stand to attention on yellow buttery icing, with four blue candles in the middle. Gemma stares. Bob strikes a match. As the children sing 'Happy Birthday, dear Gemma', she slides down in her chair, arching her stomach, blushing, avoiding their eyes, smiling — until the moment comes for her to take a huge breath, puffing out her chest. . . .

But Benjamin is there first. Quickly, with a wicked expression he blows out all four candles. Gemma has blown, too, and looks confused. But Bob and Rowena know what has happened, and angrily Bob hustles his son away from the table and out of the room. Then he relights the candles, tells the children to sing once again, so that this time Gemma can lean forward and puff out her pink cheeks — and (with the sound of her brother howling outside in her ears) become four, all on her own.

Summer

4 Donald

'Now children, we'll sing 'Maytime' — and if you let your voices go
up to the ceiling they may clear all the fog and mist away at
last. . . . Are you ready?'

'Sing a song of Maytime
Sing a song of spring,
Flowers are in their beauty,
Birds are on the wing.
Maytime, playtime,
God has given the Maytime,
Thank you for his gift of love. . . .'

Grey light filters through the roof-lights above the rows of children. The hall is high and shiny: sky-blue gloss paint and huge wall
collages of yellow and orange sunflowers compensate for the lack of
summer weather outside. At one end, behind Mrs. Eaton, the
deputy headmistress who stands facing the children, there is gym
equipment in front of a large frieze entitled, *At the Seaside*. Her voice
echoes: 'Now children, hands up any of you who know what this is
called. . . . Yes? A lifeboat, that's right. Of course this is only a
model; the real boat is about as long as this room. And who can tell
me what a lifeboat does?'

After another song the children rise and, row by row, file back to
their classrooms. The boys swing their arms in an out-of-time
march; the girls hold their heads stiffly erect to gain approval. Class
2 follows the other; Sharaz, Rekha, Rajeshiben, Pushpa, Tariq,
Zafar, Stephen, Wayne, Sarbjit, Donald, and the others, thread off
like a limb from the body of the school into their own room, under
the watchful eye of their teacher, Miss Jones. Once in the room they
rush to their own places and get out their work boxes. Each morning
it is the same. No matter what differences there are at home, Sharaz,
Rekha, Rajeshiben, Pushpa, Tariq, Zafar, Stephen, Wayne, Sarbjit,
Donald and the others know their places in the large old classroom,
know by heart the songs they sing at assembly, and know how their
teacher will organize their day.

Donald Bailey is the tallest boy in the class. He is six years old, the youngest of a family of six children. Not that all the others are children. Jackie is twenty one now, Calvin twenty, Pat eighteen, Anthony fourteen and Sonia eight. To the three oldest he is the baby they take little notice of, except for the occasional gift of 10p if they are feeling generous. To Anthony and Sonia he can be a nuisance: bursting into inexplicable tears, wanting them to play games yet not being good enough, punching the wrong button just when the programme is interesting.

Donald's parents came from Jamaica twenty-two years ago, heading for Handsworth in Birmingham, because that was where they knew people. They soon managed to buy their own house, at the end of a late Victorian terrace in Leonard Road, with small back yards in which enthusiasts try to grow flowers and bushes. For the last twenty-two years Mr Bailey has held the same job in a laminates factory. His wife works cleaning in a hospital five nights a week and spends most of the day keeping her own house clean.

Each morning Donald gets up, dresses himself quickly, eats his breakfast in the small back dining room next to the scullery, and leaves for school by 8.40. Sometimes Sonia walks with him, sometimes she doesn't – she has moved up to the juniors at Westminster Road School and does not necessarily want to be seen with her little brother. So he slips out of the house, sometimes not even bothering to say 'Good-bye' to Mrs Bailey, and scuffs along the road, turns right at the end past Najran's Cutprice Store, over the zebra crossing, across what must be the most dangerous bend in Birmingham, and finally speeds up his progress once he is in Westminster Road and sees the other children hurrying to school.

Westminster Road Infants' School is a low red-brick building in the heart of Handsworth. Its staff are paid on the special priority scale for teaching there, mainly because of the extra social problems they can expect to encounter. One or two of them joke that it is also danger money: they tend to be careful about walking home alone, especially on winter evenings, because the district has a reputation for violence.

The school draws upon the area within a tight triangle of main roads, and for the children who live there that triangle is the perimeter of the world. Once Mrs Hopkins, Donald's headmistress, discovered that some of her children did not know what an escalator was – they had never even visited the centre of Birmingham. Another time she was asked how big a cow is: 'Is it bigger than you?'

'Of *course*,' she replied – before realizing that the child had only ever seen a cow in a book or on the television.

Mrs Hopkins is a warm, energetic Welsh woman who has been teaching for thirty-one years. Sixty-five per cent of her 180 pupils are Asian, and twenty-five per cent West Indian – a startling reversal of the proportions of two or three years ago. The remaining ten per cent is half English and half Vietnamese, since a charitable organization brought the first orphans from Indo-China to Handsworth. Yet within the classrooms the different racial groups mix easily, even when they share only a few words of English as a common language. Mrs Hopkins explains: 'When the children come to my infants' school we have no racial problem at all. They all play together. But when they leave here, when they get to eight or nine, they start feeling their colour. And of course, grown-ups affect a child's thinking – and the children pick up the way they think. Which is sad, because here they are not conscious of colour. Because to us they are children. I don't care whether they're black, white, green, pink, yellow or blue – they are my children first of all. And they accept that. So while they're here it is a very protected environment.'

Donald's headmistress counts him as lucky: 'He's from a stable and well-orientated home.'

Yet no child at a school like Westminster Road Infants can escape the problems that may beset its classmates: 'On Monday many of them come in feeling tense. Quarrelling at home. A new man in the house. Mum's been out very late and the child hasn't been to bed till perhaps one in the morning. There's been arguments, there's been an unsettled air, dad has walked out, or the man has hit mother and given her a huge black eye. I have very few what you would call stable families. This is a constant presence in the school. Somewhere there is this unease, and children respond to unease. So if you have one class, like Donald Bailey's class, some of the children may have had a reasonable weekend, but there are others who come in like this' – she clenches her fists – 'uptight. You've only got to look at them the wrong way and whoosh, terrible temper. It's not their fault. They're only responding to something that's happened.

'You get children who are very naughty. Very, very naughty. They are aggressive because they are fighting for their very existence. When they're Donald's age, little minds are still wide open for you. They absorb things like sponges. The closing-in comes later. Sometimes the tension between the sort of thing they are open to at school, and the influences from around them, from the area, does depress me. And then I think to myself, if I don't do it, they'd have nothing. All right – you can show them there is another side to life. Give them the education to cope with it. You hope they are going to aim a little bit better than the people around them. That they'll know that to be black and illiterate is wicked – you are *entitled* to thump somebody. But to be black and literate – at least you can *tell* them why you're thumping them, can't you?

'A lot of people say, Poor little black children. But we have undervalued our children terrifically – black and white. We have underestimated children. I think children have far more ability, innate ability, than we've given them credit for. They have to be stretched and they do respond. The higher you expect, the better response you get. If you expect nothing, you'll get nothing. I've had mothers bring their children to school and say, Him no good child, missis, you beat him. Now if you come to school with that at four and a half, what can be your expectation?'

Mrs Hopkins runs her school on 'old-fashioned lines' – and Donald's own class teacher seems happy with the semi-formal atmosphere. No bad behaviour disturbs her routines, though this restraint does not mean that the children cannot confide in her. The one white child amongst the twenty-three was called Lara, and she came in one morning whispering that she had been to work with her mother all the night before. What sort of work? 'Ladies' work. Polishing. My mum lets me do the polishing while she does the floors. It's real ladies' work. In a big building.'

Throughout the day she would sidle up and tell her teacher that she had done five pages of writing, then seven, then ten, wanting to fill up her writing book, and wanting to be praised.

The same morning an Asian girl, her hair in plaits, also whispered something to the teacher. 'My aunt is going back to Pakistan.' The teacher made sympathetic noises – knowing that the aunt had in fact just died after a long sickness and was going home to be buried.

Donald is working on the 'School House' reading scheme. He chooses a card with pictures on it and captions beneath them which do not match. He reads the instructions carefully: 'Change the first letters of the words to two consonants that begin the name of the picture.' He frowns: the picture of a sheep has 'deep' written underneath it, and a picture of a wheel has 'feel'. Then he grins, crosses out the 'd' and inserts 'sh' – and starts work. On finishing each section of the scheme he will progress to the next one, without realizing that the violet cards test 'auditory discrimination', the tan ones, 'initial consonants', the rose ones, 'consonant combinations', and so on. Laboriously, with his mouth slightly open and his shoulders hunched, he copies the pictures into his work book and labels them correctly, until it is time for milk and biscuits, then play.

The boys burst into the yard, running, leaping high, pushing each other, stretching their arms, whirling into each other in a frenzy of pent-up energy. Games evolve: tig and tag, hide and seek around the concrete blocks that provide play corners in the yard. Donald runs and runs, without any destination, round and round, following Stephen and David, or on his own, using himself up. The girls tend to cluster in little groups, holding hands or doing strange ritualistic clapping dances; or else they cling to the hands of the teacher on playtime duty, hanging on her skirt, imparting random confidences about their lives. The older children from the junior school across the yard keep near their own building; the tiniest children in the infants congregate near the entrance to theirs, hiding from the noise and movement – or watching it, copying, waiting for the chance to be bigger too, and scatter all before.

After play, Donald's class is minded by Mrs Trevor, a 'teacher's help' with a kind face and a broad Birmingham accent. She gathers the children round her in a corner of the room, their faces expectant. 'Now, children, I think we'll get each one of you to do a turn, come up and do something like sing a song or tell a story to the rest of us.'

Hands stick into the air, fingers pointing stiffly; the boys at the back rise like a wave to attract her attention. Donald Bailey is the first. He shuffles shyly to the front, and sings 'Baa Baa Black Sheep' in a hoarse voice, through a huge grin.

Then it is Lara's turn: 'I want to do a dance – an Indian dance.' She assumes an intense expression and waves her arms jerkily in the air, long blonde hair flying. It is too much: Donald and Stephen and David, and the rest of the little knot of West Indian boys who always stick together at the back of the group, collapse on top of each other in gales of giggles. But Mrs Trevor praises Lara, reminding the class that she was remembering 'just the way the Indian lady danced,' who came to show the whole school how to do it.

The next volunteer is Sarbjit, a pretty Asian boy whose long hair is caught up into a topknot covered by a black kerchief. He stumbles over bodies to the front: 'I want to do an English dance.' His knees bend, his bottom waggles, his elbows jab the air as he bounces up and down in a parody of a go-go dancer – undeterred by the fresh wave of laughter from the back.

There is a feeling of anarchy in the air, and what is more (the children sense, rising to meet it), Mrs Trevor does not mind. She explains in an aside that she has been at the school for years, and seen the switch from permissive methods back to a more old-fashioned approach – which is what she prefers. But occasionally, she believes, it does no harm 'to let them let their hair down'.

So, 'All right, we'll all have a dance,' she says. The children leap up, laughing. 'Who can sing us a song? Who knows a song that's in the charts – on the "Top of the Pops"?'

They giggle self-consciously, until someone hits on the familiar rhythm of a song recently recorded by the Darts, and its chorus:

> 'Oooh aaah, oooh aaah, cool cool kitty,
> Talk about the boy from New York City.'

Ooohing and aaahing, ooohing and aaahing they bob up and down, flapping their arms like penguins. Then, as if she suddenly realizes that this wildness might meet with disapproval, Mrs Trevor stops them. 'All right, children, *all right*, *children*, I think we're getting too excited, all go to your seats, and I'll give you a pencil and paper so you can draw Mrs Trevor a picture.'

It is as if a jack-in-the-box were suddenly pushed slowly, awkwardly, stiffly back into its hidden crouch under the lid, untidy limbs folding, knowing nevertheless that to be locked up and wait is part of its function. So they protest only a little, and by the time Miss Jones joins them, the room is quiet again.

Shuffling home that night, Donald thought about the sudden burst of dancing. What caused it? He knows what should happen: the parcelling-up of a school's hours that makes an event like a visit from a school photographer or a student teacher an almost daring, always thrilling intrusion. So he said to his mother, 'We danced in school today.'

She said, 'Did you, boy?' but absent-mindedly, returning to her kitchen to continue her cleaning.

Donald stared at her, wondering what to do, how to fill the long light afternoon and evening. 'Can I play out?'

'In the yard, yes, but not in the road.' Mrs Bailey's reply had the weariness of a familiar formula. So Donald switched on the black and white TV in the small narrow breakfast room next to the tiny scullery, and stared mesmerized at the fuzzy images until Sonia came home from her rounders practice and took him out into the back yard to play rounders with a stick and a rolled-up newspaper ball. Their shouts echoed into the scullery, where Mrs Bailey, a plump woman who always wore a brown woollen hat pulled over her hair, talked as she cooked her chicken and rice.

'I won't let them play in the street. Not at all. It's because of the cars; and the other thing about it is they can get involved in all sorts of things. When you have a child playing in the back yard you don't have to worry, because you know exactly where they are – on their own, or if their special friends are there. But in the street they can meet up with so many different lots. Next thing you know, somebody will be ringing my bell – my little boy breaking a window or something. So I don't like them playing in the street. I don't think it's the place for them. Then you read these things, like this week, those two children killed that old woman. Babies – one of them was six, the same as Donald. I think it's horrible. I can't say anything about it because I don't know all the background – but you have to be thinking of things like that, I hate that – the violence.

'Some parents round here have a problem with their kids. Some don't. Everywhere you go, it's the same. But I've had no trouble with my children. Jackie, Pat, Calvin, they all do well. And Anthony does all the sports – he's very proud of himself. I hope Donald will be the same. Because if he got into trouble it would break my heart. It would break my heart – this is one thing I'm not looking forward to – getting himself involved in things like that. It would break my heart.

'You have to bring your children up the best way you can, and hope for the best. You've got some control over it, while they are in your house. But outside. . . .' She shook her head dubiously. 'Well, it's not just you, is it? Kids are influenced by their home, but sometimes it's a bad home. Sometimes they are influenced by friends, and things like that. All you do, you let your children know that you don't like that sort of thing. Whether they like it or not, just let them know you don't stand for nonsense. But I don't think you should plan for them too much. Donald is six, it's too early for him to know what he will be. I believe when a child has plans, like to be a teacher, a photographer, a policeman, I think he will make a good job of it because he is interested in it. But if you want your child to be a teacher just to please mum and dad, he won't do it. So all you do is tell them to make the most of their education. That's all you can do.

'When you think of it – you wonder when you are younger if you will be able to have kids. Or what it will be like. Once you start having kids, you love them more and more, and you are so worried about them. I wonder now what the next few years will be for these children. And my grandchildren. This is something everybody is thinking about. Things are going the other way around. Bad. Kids more uncontrolled. Now in my home it was not like that. I would go home to Jamaica tomorrow, because there is no place like home. I do miss home, though I have been here for twenty two years. But my kids have never been there. This is home to them. And I want them to get on here. But as I said, up to now, I haven't had any problems.

'Pat works for a firm that makes badges and things, and Jackie works in an office, and Calvin works at this sheetmetal place. I am proud of them. It's nothing much to be proud of, really. My home isn't the best, but it's not the worst. It could be better, really. Still, we accept it as our home. It don't let us down. And I give my children pocket money, so they don't have to ask nobody, and don't have to pinch things, like biscuits or sweets. If they come to ask me for something I am willing to give it to them. I live by certain principles – like not asking people for things, and I don't want them to let me down. My children can ask *me*. I don't mind them asking me. I want my children to be . . . I try to give them family life. I don't want them to feel they're cut off. I'm still mum.'

That night, as every other, Donald played with Sonia and watched TV, until at about 11 p.m. he fell asleep in his chair and his father carried him upstairs to bed.

The next morning he arrived at school to find that Miss Jones was ill. Already Mrs Hopkins had made arrangements to cope, by putting in Mrs Canning to teach Donald's class and distributing her own class throughout the school.

Her style was very different to that of their class teacher; gayer, more confident. She asked mental arithmetic questions in a swift pattern – 'If you had eleven flowers in your garden and a naughty boy came along and took two, how many would you have left?' – and the hands shot up eagerly. When she said she would give out 'sum cards' – 'What sort do you want, easy ones or hard ones?' – Donald and Lara and Stephen and Pushpa and most of the class shouted, 'Hard ones, Mrs Canning, hard ones!'

After play, she decided to gather them in a corner of the room to have a discussion about friendship – the school theme of the week.

Jason, a poorly dressed, slightly sad-looking white child from Mrs Canning's own class, put up his hand and said that he had a best friend. 'Come and tell us about it.' Standing shyly next to her he spoke of a secret den down a long garden (longer than any real garden in Handsworth) where he had a den and played games with his best friend. He would not name the friend or describe the garden . . . only that 'they' would not allow girls into the secret place. He said the gang had a leader – and immediately his voice was drowned by a hubbub: Donald and his friends shouting things together.

'Don't all talk at once – what are you saying? Put your hand up if you'd like to be a leader.' Like most of them, Donald put up his hand, but Jason's hands stayed pulling at the frayed wool of his stained pullover. 'Don't you want to be a leader, Jason?' asked Mrs Canning gently. He shook his head gloomily, and said no more.

Mrs Canning hauled Donald up before the class to tell them about his best friend. He grinned with embarrassment: 'His name begins with S. He is in this class. He is wearing a red jumper with blue trousers and blue socks and black and white pumps. He's nearly seven, I think. He's bigger than me. . . .'

By this time boys were nudging Stephen, the West Indian boy who was in fact smaller than Donald but who was always in the midst of that particular group of boys.

'Why is he your friend?'

'Because . . . he laughs too much.'

'Is that why you like him? You like people who laugh? Why?'

'He's happy . . . it makes you happy.'

'All right, let's have him up here with you. Stephen, who is your best friend?'

There is no hesitation, no thought for form. 'David,' he said decisively.

'But you play with Donald,' prompted Mrs Canning quickly.

'Yes, and Paul, and Adrian, and Sarbjit.'

Donald said, 'Stephen is the boss of our gang. David is the second boss. I'm the third boss.'

'No, you're not,' shouted Paul and David. 'You're the fourth boss.'

Stephen said, 'I decided that David would be second boss and Wayne would be third boss.'

Mrs Canning was clearly fascinated, like the rest of the class. It was as if a very private thing they had suspected was suddenly being aired in public, and no one wanted to miss the gossip.

'What does Stephen do, Donald?'

'He's a good boss. He decides what game we play. And who is in the gang. He tells Wayne he's not a good boss.'

Stephen added, 'I think *he* should be boss number three, and Wayne should be boss number four.' Donald preened slightly, grinning at the class as if to say they should have known his worth. The boy Wayne was absent.

'But what will Wayne say, Stephen, if he comes back and finds you've put him down to number four?'

'Oh, he keeps telling us he's going to Jamaica.'

Donald added, 'His daddy's got a shop in Jamaica.'

'What does it sell?'

'Coconuts,' they shouted derisively.

'Now, tell me what you'd do, Stephen, if boss number four suddenly decided he wanted to be boss number one?'

Donald muttered, 'You must be joking.'

'So, Donald, you don't want to be boss number one?'

'No.'

'Do you like being boss number four?'

'No.'

'Do you want to be boss number three?'

'*Yes.*'

Stephen turned to Mrs Canning with the air of someone explaining a fact to a foreigner. 'He is already boss number three, because I've just decided.'

'What I don't understand is why you think it's necessary to have all these bosses. Why can't you just all be in the gang?'

There is silence for a moment. The boys looked at each other, and even Lara piped up inconsequentially, 'Paul is boss number five, Mrs Canning,' as if to show that she too could not understand such a question.

'Bosses tell you what to do,' rasps Donald in his hoarsest voice.

'Yes, but . . . why do you all have to be bosses — is it so if boss numbers one and two are away, boss number three will tell the others what to do?'

'*Yes,*' yelled the four boys in chorus, as if she were stupid. And the young teacher had to give up the struggle, defeated by the children's assurance that hierarchies are at the root of co-existence, that each boy has to know his particular part of the chain. . . .

At playtime, as always, the gang hung out around the concrete blocks — with Sarbjit the only non-West Indian amongst them. Donald and Stephen were practising kung fu kicks, narrowly missing each other's faces. At dinner time they shared the same table, eating their meat pie, potatoes, cabbage and gravy in comparative silence, walking out separately without addressing a word to each other, then suddenly forming their little exclusive group, talking, planning, pushing, playing tig and tag outside under the sky. Later Donald said: 'We had a proper meeting at dinner time. We said that Wayne is out of the gang altogether, and I'm boss number three now. Stephen said so – at the meeting.' He added that he did not care a bit about Wayne.

At lunch time Mrs Canning watched them from the staffroom window – running hither and thither, ceaselessly, with nowhere to go. She said: 'People talk about the resilience of children, but at the age of six I think it is just innocence, really. They don't know about what life holds in store for them. They don't know much – and so it's possible for them to be happy.'

Donald was bored. First Sonia had refused to play rounders with him because he was far below her standard; then Anthony had made a joke at his expense over tea, then . . . there was nothing to play with, the sun was shining outside, the house throbbed to Calvin's reggae, Mr B. was cutting the hedge, Mrs B. cleaning the kitchen as always, the television picture was poor, and anyway there was nothing on. . . .

'We could go to Handsworth Park,' said Anthony, kicking a ball from one foot to the other in the narrow passage.

Handsworth Park, notorious in reputation, beautiful in aspect, lies about fifteen minutes' walk from the Bailey's house. There are tall wrought-iron gates, well-kept lawns, a stream with ornamental bridges, playgrounds, packed flower-beds, and an extraordinary absence of litter.

The evening is summery, with only the slightest chill in the air although it is six o'clock. Couples stroll arm in arm, and gangs of boys play football on the flat plateaux. There are no white people anywhere in the park. Classes from Donald's school used to go there regularly, but Mrs Hopkins stopped that. She decided that episodes of violence in the park at night made it unwise to go there: white people had been attacked, and she was concerned for the safety of her teachers and children. It was the same concern that prompted her winter rule that no member of staff must be in the school building after 4.30 p.m. Such concern is understandable, but so is the regret of people like the Westminster's West Indian home-school liaison officer Hazel Wright who feels that such white caution isolates, that the inevitable black response will be one of non-serious or serious aggression. But tonight the park is totally peaceful.

Anthony, last year's West Midlands Under 14 cross-country champion, and Sonia, of Westminster Junior School rounders team, and Donald, boss number three, walk about two yards apart from each other, speaking little, glad of each other's company, yet too separate in their years and ability to be able to play with each other. So they adopt family roles. When Donald climbs too high on the dangerous climbing tower, where lithe teenage boys swing and fight, Anthony bellows for him to come down. Sonia watches him too. And when she strays too far Anthony shouts for her to return as well, so that the three of them grow frustrated: each wanting to go off, yet needing to stay together. On the seesaw Anthony is too heavy, so Sonia and Donald sit together on one side, to make up the weight.

The only time the silent Anthony unbends is to tease Donald and call him 'a bad man'.

'I'm not,' protests the little boy.

'Yes, you are, you bad man' – and Sonia and Anthony tease him in chorus, throwing the football to bounce off his back, capering round him, holding him at arms' length when he tries to throw a futile punch.

But when Anthony finds a stray football on the grass and appropriates it, Donald is proud. 'If that man came whose ball that is and said he wanted it, Tuni would fight him. He'd beat him too.' So the three of them walk along, looking for things to do, Anthony carrying his own football, with the new one tucked hilariously under his track suit top, as the evening grows cooler and the shadows longer. The park is quiet – a seemingly endless expanse of golden-green and rustling shade in which even the deeper shouts of a group of young men playing football fade into insignificance.

When they arrive home at about nine o'clock, their mother is watching the news. It is followed by a Conservative Party political broadcast, causing Mrs B. to raise her eyes to heaven and fold her arms.

Donald watches in amazement: 'They're walking backwards. Why are they walking backwards, Tuni?' Anthony tells him that they are running the film backwards. 'But people don't walk backwards,' says Donald, staring open-mouthed at the screen.

Indeed, planes are flying backwards, ships are plunging backwards through their own foam, and a climber reverses down the mountain he has just been climbing. Then people, or rather actors, stand in a mock-dock and admit that they are 'guilty' for wanting to buy their own home, or a Sunday joint, or a holiday. . . . 'That's *silly*,' says Donald.

Mrs Bailey huddles more into the fold of her own arms: 'I am not interested in this. This politics. They all the same to me. They promise you everything just to get your vote, and then they do nothing. When they are in they are getting their fat salaries, and they forget you. And these people, didn't Mrs Thatcher say she wanted black people to go? I think she did. It not worth bothering with them. That's how it seems to me.' Donald, huddled against his mother, is falling asleep.

On Thursday, Mr Bailey went to the doctor and heard the news that on Monday he could return to work. For a few months he had been off sick, because of a rash on his hands and arms caused by chemicals used at his factory. 'I've been fed up – sittin' around. For twenty-two years I work in that place, and I can't wait to get back there.' Mr Bailey, a tall burly man with greying hair habitually covered by a flat black leather cap, is a charge hand in the inspection department at the laminates factory, and will detail with pride the processes that are used, the different requirements of different customers, and so on. In their rarely used front room, over the gleaming glass, chrome, and Formica sideboard, and amongst the studio portraits of Calvin, Pat and Jackie as toddlers, hangs a photograph of a much younger Mr Bailey, in his work overalls, in front of an instrument board.

'I'm lucky in my job. I like my work – it interests me. We all get along so good at work. Nothing bothers me that much. I never have any bother with people because I'm coloured, not at my work. I get along all right. I know fellows that have trouble, but my personal self – no. If I tell you anybody ever look at me or call me names I would tell a lie. I work at my place for several years and they make me the head of our little group there, and there's only one coloured man with me. All the rest of the fellows is white. And they always handle me quite nice. And I always handle them quite nice, as well. I could be one of the lucky ones in that kind of way.

'We are all in the T & G, and I always vote for the Labour Party – but I'm not interested in politics, not much. Whether they do good or bad I just keep voting. I don't change. . . . So far – I think I understand myself. I'm not always right, you know, I must remember that. I got to do things wrong as well, because I'm only human. I'm not going to praise myself. But I think that home training is really a good thing in a person's life. After leaving home in Jamaica when I was about nineteen I travelled to the United States. I met a lot of people, fellows, and we all worked together. And I could see the difference. A person who had a good home trainin' and somebody without – it was two different things. I got to take up my pen and wrote my mother and father a letter and thanked them for what they had done for me.

'My dad was a baker – he was a very strict man. He never let me play in the street in Jamaica, and I don't let my kids play in the street here. I had respect for my dad – until I was twenty-one I wouldn't ever smoke in front of him. . . . But kids today, they don't have that respect. It is all around – the influences on them. I don't see much what you can really do about it. Only talk to them. Show them the right way. What you believe is right – and if they hear what you have to say, that's good. If not, well, I don't think you can do much about it by the time they sixteen or seventeen. Donald is little now, he's at school. He's getting on good. He's picked up his lessons. Then you start thinkin', plannin' you'd like him to be something or other. . . . You can't get along without education. So I let him know what I think about that. A lot of things must come from the parents. As I said, the home is where they grows up!

'I can see a lot of things that happen around here, with the kids, and the parents doesn't care – just let them go like that. After a while they become criminals. I feel sorry for the kids because the parents isn't taking any notice of them. . . . If you have your kids you've got to be interested in them because you would like them to be somebody worthwhile.'

Like his wife, Mr Bailey misses Jamaica, although he is contented to live in Handsworth: 'I was in the United States, and then I go back home, and people were coming over here. So I wanted to come. Maybe because it's in me – you gain a lot of experience from travellin'. Learn a lot. Things you'd never thought of, you have seen with your own eyes. Things that you'd read in books. So I came here, and I came straight to Handsworth, and I've never been away since.

'My intention was always to go home, really. I must tell the truth – there's no place like home. I can remember my days at home, and I enjoyed it. Even some of my friends back home, old schoolmates, well, a lot of them is better off than me now. If I went back I would be poorer than them now. Sometimes I feel sorry that I come to England, and sometimes I don't. My kids done all right, and I did . . . but it is the money. You always have to worry about money.

You don't get a holiday. And I see the kids leave school here and expect to earn as much money as me. You can't do that. You have to work up to things, and save your money. My children work all the day — that's what I say about the kids who don't work; perhaps if their parents did, they would. Because I always worked hard all the days of my life. My wife too — she always do that. Kids — they are a lot of responsibility. . . .'

Donald has come home from school, and has crept into the front room. He has been listening to his father talk for the last ten minutes.

Mr B: 'What you going to be when you grow up?'

Donald: 'A fire engine.'

Mr B: 'You have to grow wheels.'

Donald: 'A fire engine man! I like to go down that thing you slide down. I have to get more money than my dad.'

Mr B: 'You want to get more money than me! I tell my kids, if you stick here you can save a lot of money. Calvin, if he saves he will have a lot of money when he's twenty-five. I tell him, don't get married — you save. Mind you, I can't save. Perhaps when they all grow up I do better. Now Donald, he don't save his pocket money, do you?'

Donald: 'No. I did once. I save forty, fifty pence. Then I asked you to buy me fish and chips, remember? And you wouldn't, so. . . .'

Mr B: 'That's what I give you money for — to buy your own fish and chips. That's what it's for!'

Donald: 'You give me money because I work. At the dustbins — I have to do it on Saturday, so you give me money.'

Mr B: 'And you tell me you want a rise.'

Donald: 'I had 5p when I was four, and 10p when I was five, and now I get 15p, and I want a rise to twenty. No — I want a pound!'

Mr B: 'Now you goin' too far. Too far. You got to do some more work.'

Donald: 'You don't work. You only stand around outside and go to people's houses.'

Mr B: 'That's my privilege. I been workin' hard all my life. Anyway, I've been sick with my skin. But I'm going on Monday now.'

Donald: 'That's good. You have to get more rise.'

Mr B: 'Because if I get more money, you be better off, hey?'

Donald: 'Yes.'

Mr B: 'Oh, he gets away with anything, this boy. The older ones, I was more strict with them, and they went to Sunday school and all that. But now ... well, six kids is a lot to bring up. I didn't really have any intention of having all these kids. It's a handful. A lot to keep. But I still keep them.'

In school that day, Donald had read this to his teacher, moving his finger laboriously along the line under the words, his voice an expressionless monotone:

'John — saw — a — big — aeroplane. — He — walked — up — to — it — with — father. — The — man — in — the — aeroplane — said, — "Do — you — want — to — fly?" — "Yes — please," — said — John, — "I — want — to — come — with — you." — "Get — in — then," — said — the — man.' — Father — and — John — got — in. — Mother — stood — and — looked. — "Good-bye — mother," — said — John.'

At home that evening, he wandered from the front room into the scullery to tell his mother something. He said that all he wanted was a bicycle. Mrs B. wiped her hands on her trousers, shaking her head: 'A bicycle! I'd like to buy you a bicycle, I really would, boy. But I haven't got the money. When your birthday comes, I haven't got the money to get you anything much at all, and that's the truth. It's Jackie's birthday next week, and I can't buy her nothing. All the money goes, boy, and that's the truth.'

Later, Donald sat with Sonia and his mother on the old settee, waiting for 'Top of the Pops' on the TV. As always the music blasted from Calvin's room – this time the Handsworth Band, 'Steel Pulse'. When the programme came on it bored them – the girl dancers posturing to poor rhythms, the gutless sound of punk boys pretending to be angry, the attempts at folk emotion.

Every five minutes Mrs B. would shake her head, and mutter, 'This rubbish.'

'But there's one mum likes,' beamed Sonia, 'there's one coming mum likes, and we all like.'

At last it was the end of the programme and time for the number one: 'The Rivers of Babylon', by the West Indian group called Boney M. Mrs B. grinned.

> 'By the rivers of Babylon,
> Where we sat down,
> There we wept,
> When we remembered Zion. . . .'

They all joined in the words – 'Oh, how shall we sing the Lord's song in a strange land' – Donald and Sonia in their Birmingham accents, whilst their mother nodded her head to the music.

5 Andrew

With his black mask on at the fair he is a pirate, snarling and cruel —
roughly jolting a little girl's gas-filled balloon out of her hand, so
that it vanishes into the clouds and she cries. After watching 'The
Incredible Hulk' he is transformed, small shoulders broadening,
arms lengthening, an inarticulate roar escaping from his lips as he
attacks the gold velvet sofa in a fury, and his mother tells him please
to behave himself.

At other times he is less formidable. Once when his parents were
downstairs working he crept from his bed and along the corridor to
the pink spare bedroom. Opening the door silently he saw it: the tall
shadow looming over the far twin bed, wavering, bending across the
ceiling towards him. And he fled back to his own room, knowing
what he would never tell his parents, that the ghost waits for anyone
who ventures into that little room alone.

Andrew Hill, seven years old, with his straight reddish hair and
freckles, lives out his fantasy life in his parents' public house in
Liverpool. Not that the residents of Woolton like to think of themselves as being a part of the big, sprawling, rough and lively city.
Woolton, they explain, has always been a village, on the outskirts of
the city, but with its own character and population. They may even
romanticise the place, resenting slightly the fact that high-rise flats
now loom over the 'village', and the city has engulfed it like a
voracious organism.

In the last century Woolton had its share of social problems, and
contained the same social mix as it does today. Irish labourers'
families crowded into one-up-one-down terraces in Quarry Street
and Pit Street, whilst their young women (if they were lucky) served
the gentry in Woolton Hall and other big houses. Now the opulent
bungalows of Woolton Park, at least one of them with three Rolls-
Royces in the garage, belong to *nouveau riche*; the gentry have
departed, and the village still contains the children of the labouring
poor, still working for a living — if jobs can be found on Merseyside.
Andrew's headmaster, at Bishop Martin Church of England School,
insists upon a school uniform because, he says, the school contains

such a diversity of children, from such varying economic backgrounds, that a uniform serves to minimize the difference between
rich and poor.

The Derby Arms Hotel serves both. Colin and Jean Hill are the
tenants, owning all the fixtures and fittings, paying the brewery a
rent, and running a 'profitable little business'. Standing on the busy
Allerton Road, the pub has never been modernized with brass and
plastic, but stays as modest as it was when they started over ten years
ago. The outside badly needs painting; the inside is plain. Only a
shiny fruit machine punctuates the conversation of the regulars with
its perpetual tinkle and thump. Andrew's first steps were taken in
the lounge bar. When he was three he could hand the barmaid any
bottle of any kind of beer she asked for, picking it from the low
shelves behind the bar, knowing the different beers from the colours
of their labels. He used to say he wanted to work in a pub when he
grew up, and loved to sit on the knees of the customers at dinner
time, pocketing their 5ps for packets of crisps.

Now he is apt to dismiss the pub. Once he remonstrated with his
teacher, Mrs Quin, when she mentioned to the class that he lived
over a pub: 'It's not a pub, it's a hotel.' In theory he was right,
though no passerby could find a room there. Jean and Colin live on
one floor over the rooms which pay them, with three bedrooms, two
sitting rooms and a large modern kitchen with microwave oven,
electric deep fryer and other conveniences. Each year the Hills take
Andrew on a skiing holiday, and they both have a car. Though
Andrew might be half-ashamed of the fact that he lives over a pub,
Colin and Jean congratulate themselves that all the years of hard
work have paid off, and that they have achieved their joint ambition
to be successful in a small business.

They met when Jean was sixteen; he worked as a plasterer, she as a
typist. For six years they 'courted' but when they finally married
they decided not to have any children until they had 'got on their
feet'. Colin did not want to remain a plasterer, nor Jean a typist.
Though not ashamed of their own backgrounds they wanted to do
better, to work for themselves. They spent five and a half years
building up the business in a little backstreet pub, paid a wage by
the brewery, then came to the Derby Arms. After three years, with
business going well, they finally decided they could afford to have a
child – much to the delight of Colin's mother, who had waited a
long time for her first grandchild.

Each Wednesday Colin and Jean take the day off, dress up in their
best clothes and go out. Perhaps they drive to Wales or Yorkshire;

they just like to get away from the pub. On those days Andrew's grandparents come round to give him his tea and look after him until, at about 11 p.m., Jean and Colin come back. Millie and George Hill are in their seventies, and they look forward to their weekly babysitting duty. Millie is indulgent with her grandson: 'Yes, his nanna comes every Wednesday – and he really likes me coming, even though I say it myself. I read him a chapter of his book when he's in bed.

'Once I looked in his diary. I know I shouldn't have done, but I wanted to know about his little life – what he put. And it was harmless little things – what he did. Children don't do much. But one Wednesday he'd put, My nanny comes to my house at 12 noon – he'd put 'noon' just like that! And on another Wednesday he'd put, I will go home quickly because my nanny will be at our house. It's nice that they – like – value those funny things. I wonder if it will last, though. I know it sounds old fashioned, and I don't know if Jean and Colin would agree with me, but I'd like to keep children in their . . . purity and innocence. But it's hard these days. In my day you could a bit longer. But they grow up so fast now. It's the television and things like that. You can't stop it. But . . . I'd like to hold on to that . . . er . . . sweetness longer. It goes . . . Andrew is a lovely boy, but he's getting a big boy now. He's only seven, but the other day he said to me, I've got all hairs on me arms, nan, why is that? I know it has to go. So he doesn't come to you, like he did. Big boys don't give cuddles to their nanna.'

Colin Hill's father taught his son his own trade. Now Colin stands behind the bar, puffing his pipe, dressed in a well cut beige suit and a wide, coloured tie, and says that like his own father, he wants 'more' for his son.

'I'd rather my lad did even better than me. To think, instead of, me mam and dad did this; well, I'll do a bit better than them. See, I don't want Andrew to deal with the public. I don't want him to see trouble. I've thrown a lot of people out, I've learned to deal with trouble before it starts. I could get bashed over the head, or coshed for the till. It might only have £15 in it or £500, but I don't want to see him in that position. I rather my lad became a doctor, or something like that – a family doctor.

'So I want him to do well at school, though I don't put pressure on him. As regards education, as regards maths, or what schooling means – I don't know. I left school at fifteen, admitted, and wasn't the brightest – but my maths was far simpler and far better. My lad would have been a lot better off on the old methods: 315 plus 214, add them up, tens and units – all that. Mental arithmetic – I say to him, Andrew, what's 315 multiplied by 10? He can do it, he says you just add a nought, and if it's by a hundred you add two noughts. Well, they don't teach them that at school. I still have to do maths now – I get the cigarettes in, or the stock, and I have to add it up – two lines at the bottom and the figure put in. And he will . . . whether he's paying out bills, or sending bills in the future, wherever the hell he is in life – I think he'll get bills in the same way, y' know? It's got to go at the bottom between two lines whether you're paying them out or collecting them in. You have to know maths because it makes your mind think. Anybody that can do maths is good. Now I think that if in school they had the old thing – adding up, all in columns, hundreds, tens and units, down to the bottom, my lad would be better off. As it is, he can't put it down on paper.

'I once asked him what he wanted to do in life. He said that he wanted to run a pub. I wouldn't like to encourage him in that. We spoke about it you know. So I said, what else would you like to do? And he said, 'I'd like to be an artist.' Afterwards I thought, well, if that's what he wants, I'll encourage him to do that. Oh, I don't really want to have any influence on him, none at all.

'You know it makes us laugh, Jean and me. People think that we must be so busy we don't have time for our lad. Well, I've seen more of my lad since he's been born and until he went to school than most people do. When he comes home from school now he rings the bell, and he says, dad, where's mum? and I say, She's out at the shops, or something like that. But it's always dad this and dad that. Sometimes he calls me Colin – we're more that way. At the same time, I play hell with him. He puts his point of view to me and I choke him off. I do really tell him off. At the same time, he comes and explains things to me. He'll still defy me sometimes – why I don't know. But it's all right – the way he is. He's our lad. He goes to school and comes home, and does everything on his own. He gets his own breakfast. If you wanted to help him you couldn't. That's the way the lad is – so I've never stopped him. He's a quiet lad, but I think he's all right. Look – we work hard. I've always worked hard. And Jean and Andrew – I've always seen them all right. That's all I live for. Though I wouldn't tell her that and I don't think she'd tell me.'

Andrew dresses himself in his grey uniform in the morning, yells, 'Where's me belt? Where is it, mam?', cleans his black shoes, eats his sausage buttie in the living room, before walking on his own to school. Bishop Martin School is a new building, lying by the side of St Peter's Church with its crumbling, over-populated graveyard. The headmaster, Mr McCoskery, shows the visitor round his school with pride — pointing out that in the junior department each child is working at its own pace at different activities and yet there is no hubbub. He believes that the open-plan layout and flexible methods teach his pupils independence and concentration, and considers the standards in his school equal to any school in the city.

There are thirty children in Andrew's class. Though their teacher, Mrs Quin, has no formal classroom, she has a 'home base' on one corner of the large open-plan infants' section, to which she can retire with her class, pulling a yellow concertina partition across after her. A similar system can separate the other three classes in the area, with the centre space shared. Although Mrs Quin has been teaching for thirty seven years she calmly accepts the new style of education that is so different from the 'talk and chalk' of her first school experience. Yes, she says, the children develop, and although 'it can get noisy', they are stimulated to find things out for themselves. Since they moved to the new building, she thinks their reading has actually improved.

The date, 29 June, is chalked on the board. The children copy it into their 'News and Story' books. 'Come on now, Darren, you know your work book is in your box,' shouts Mrs Quin above the gentle buzz to a small boy who is wandering aimlessly around the room. One side of the 'home base' consists of a plate-glass window, on which shapes of butterflies and flowers are pasted, making a garden through which the view of towering flats and factory chimneys looks unreal. Rivulets of rain run down around the coloured shapes; the sky is grey.

By mid-morning Andrew, sitting at a table with his friend, Finn McGough (son of the poet, Roger McGough), is copying numbers neatly into his maths book from a green sum card. In the room the boys and girls form separate groups, since the children can sit where they wish and the sexes never choose to sit together. When a child has finished he or she takes the book to Mrs Quin who sits in a corner — she does not have a conventional teacher's desk. The books flutter round her, voices clamour for her attention as she hears one child read, marks another's sums, sets yet another an exercise to do from a book which tests comprehension, tells another where to go next in a reading scheme, and so on.

Through it all, Andrew Hill works quietly. He rarely chatters and plays around like the other boys on his table. Jean Hill gave him careful instruction when he first went to school that he must always finish his work, ask for no help, and not be distracted. He seems to have taken it to heart. Mrs Quin is clearly fond of him: 'He's a good, well-adjusted little boy. A very good little worker altogether.'

When the children spill outside into the general area, to work at measuring or drawing with more space, or when they return from lunch, they always take a different place. Their work boxes are kept in a chest outside the 'home base' so there is nothing to identify them in the room. For some of them, this presents a problem. Andrew himself tends to gravitate to the same chair he was sitting on before, but if he finds it is already occupied he moves away without a word. But a tall boy called Mark objects. Twice during one day he takes Mrs Quin aside, and asks for the system (or lack of it) to be changed. 'Wouldn't it save us getting muddled up if we each had a chair with our name on?'

But Mrs Quin tells him it does not matter where he sits, and comments: 'The children squabble over chairs. One of the things that is hard to instil in them with the open plan is that they haven't got one place – they haven't their *own* place.'

Position is not the only worry for Mark. Mrs Quin knows that he has a disabled sibling who receives all the attention at home. One afternoon when she allows them to play with toys, a group of boys grab the Lego box. Andrew sits down to construct a sort of battleship, with infinite patience. Finn and the others grab bits more wildly to build oddly shaped houses and towers, fighting good-humouredly for a particularly useful brick, but collaborating on their building. Mark tries to join in but, defeated, picks up some bricks to make his own model. It is small, and indefinable. The others laugh at him – 'Mark's making a rubber dinghy', 'Mark's making a sausage roll', 'Mark's making a flea'.

Andrew takes no notice, building his control tower, muttering, 'That's where the men with the guns go.' But he is using too many bricks.

When Mrs Quin notices that Mark has none, she intervenes: 'I think you boys should work together a bit. You have to share things. Mark, perhaps Andrew would appreciate you putting a few bricks on his model?' Her voice is cajoling, but Andrew moves his model away, turning his back on the others, horrified at the suggestion. And Mark rushes off in tears – pursued unobtrusively a few minutes later by Mrs Quin, who sets him to tidy a cupboard and promises that he can have first go on the Lego next time.

Andrew's books are neat. Everything he does is approached in the same methodical fashion. But surprisingly, his 'News' book contains no news at all. Leila and Finn and Paul and Darren and the others tend to write in what they did at the weekend, what their mum bought them, or who came to tea. Not Andrew. To look at his book you would think that the exciting world of the pub, and his mum and dad, and his nanna and his holidays, did not exist. This was one of his stories:

One upon a time there was a big big big big big big giant he lived in a big big big big big big big big BIG castel and he was very sad because it was always winter and outside his gardan it was very sunny wher the little peple lived like us and when he came outside it just raind and he had to go into his castel and then he let the boys and girls like us go into his gardan and then the sun shone and that was the end of the story.

Mrs Quin wrote 'and what a lovely story!', and gave him a star.

When Andrew marches home he switches on the TV, still in his school uniform, and waits for his tea. Jean is usually in the kitchen, Colin downstairs, supervising something in the pub. One night they are visited by Millie Hill and Colin's two sisters, and Andrew pummels his favourite Aunt Audrey, ten years younger than Colin, whose face shows the strain of being involved in a nasty divorce after a violent marriage. Andrew leaps on her, throwing an old coat over her head, while his mother and grandmother protest and she laughs, if wearily. But he is gentle with Audrey's two-year-old daughter: 'Come and sit down, come on,' he says, in the tone of voice able-bodied adults reserve for the old and disabled.

When they have left, and Andrew sits down with his parents in the kitchen to eat his meal of steak, chips and vegetables, he tells Jean and Colin the story of the Child of Hale – a real-life giant called John Middleton who lived centuries before on the outskirts of Liverpool. Mrs Quin had told the class his story days earlier, and each child had made large coloured cutouts of the 'Child' to be fixed to the notice board.

Jean and Colin are interested. But suddenly Jean asks: 'What did you do with those tables I typed out for you – do you know them yet?' Andrew takes another mouthful so that he cannot speak. He shakes his head. 'Come on, Andrew, where are they?'

He has to make a reply: 'I drawed on the back of them,' he says, grinning and growing pink.

'Oh, Andrew, I'm wasting me time,' says Jean.

Jean Hill is a matter-of-fact sort of person who hides behind enormous gilt spectacles, and matches her clothes carefully. She makes no fuss of her son, but calls him 'matey' and would not dream of going away on their package holidays to Switzerland without him.

'I couldn't be without him now. He's good company. The three of us, we go out on Sundays to Ainsdale beach, places like that, and we have some good times. But I wouldn't have another one. Another child. I might have done ... but I had such an awful time with Andrew, a terrible time. I had a caesarean − lots of trouble, you know. I couldn't be bothered now. I wouldn't mind one for company for him, but I couldn't go through all that again.

'I don't think being an only child has any effect on anybody whatsoever. I'm one of four. Colin's one of three. I was basically on my own, really. People say he must get lonely, but I think it's a load of rubbish. Well, I mean, if you bring your child up to feel he's dependent on you, and he's the only one, and he has this attitude whereby he can't do anything, you've always got to do things for him and play with him − then I suppose he will get lonely. But if you bring him up to mix with other people, go and find his friends and do the things he wants to do, I don't think he'll ever be lonely. He goes out and plays. I say to him, You're going out − where are you going? and he says, I'm going to Philip's, or, I'm going to the park or whatever, and I let him run off. He used to talk a lot to the customers in the pub, sit and chat, but now he doesn't want to know. Well, he just wants to play with children now.'

Andrew's mother shares her husband's preoccupation with the learning of mathematics, and talks about tens and units with regret − although she emphasises that she likes Bishop Martin School. One thing she is sure of − she does not want him to go to a comprehensive when he leaves his junior school.

'Why? Because I don't like them, that's all. But I don't know if he'll be right enough to go to the Bluecoat − they have boarders there − well, they did do. I don't know if they still do; I don't know if they have to win a scholarship to get there, I really and truly don't. I haven't looked into it enough. As regards going to a comprehensive, I think the children are rough − but I don't really know if it would have an effect on him. It's just a thing I've got on my mind. But we've always had choice in this country and all of a sudden it's taken away from us. Our freedom has gone. So we've thought about paying for him. As things stand at the present time, yes, we can afford it. But school fees don't stand still. As the children get older the fees get more expensive. I mean, the dentist we go to, it was costing him £1000 a year or something, to send his children. He had three children at school. Well, he just couldn't afford it and had to take the two youngest ones away. I'd hate to start Andrew off like that and not be able to finish it. So I just don't know what to do. I try not to think about the future. He's too young. Not at seven years of age . . .

'But I'd hate him to be a layabout like we've got today. Hanging about on the streets doing nothing. There are thousands of them. It'll never be any different when they can get money for doing nothing. What incentive is there for them to work? They get money for doing nothing so they're not going to work, are they? I hate it. Makes me mad. I think it's dreadful. And when they do go to work they're so idle they're useless. I daren't think about the future. But you think about communism and you think about the Russians, and they infiltrate here, there and everywhere. It's a bit frightening. I'm not really interested in politics, but everyone's affected. I should hate to see England become a communist state. After all, our dads and grandads have fought two world wars, so I can't see. . . . But you don't know. What's the point of it? What does it matter? The children didn't have any choice about coming into the world. You don't get any choice. You go to the school your parents want you to go to – and you're not old enough to know whether *you* want to go there or not. All of us – it's the same. You're just born to it.'

Unaware of his mother's anxieties Andrew slips off from the pub, carrying his skateboard under one arm. He walks down a narrow side road to where a gnarled old tree, set in its own raised brick-walled plot of soil, shadows the pavement, though dwarfed by the looming block of flats immediately behind it. The tree becomes a den; or a base to which the boys flee back. Three other boys are already perched on the dusty brick wall, under the branches. One of them, a tall, plump boy with cropped fair hair, is also called Andrew. He is nine. His friend, a pale, thin boy, who says that his 'house' is somewhere different from the place he 'stays', is called Stephen – who, though much smaller, is actually ten. With them, dragging along wherever they go, is Stephen's five-year-old brother Neil. The three boys are dressed in jeans and T-shirts; Andrew still wears his uniform.

Andrew's skateboard is the common interest. They discuss its merits, big Andrew making excuses for the fact that he has not brought his ('The ball bearings have come out. It was too cheap.') in order to persuade little Andrew to hand over his. And he does. His own attempts were stumbling and slow. The bigger boy shows off on the skateboard in the middle of the road – to the irritation of two passing old ladies who shout that he will get run over. 'You can get them that you sit on. You can get them jet-propelled in America,' shouts big Andrew, trying to do a 'quarter turn'.

'Well, it wouldn't be a skateboard then, would it?' replies Stephen and, exercising the rights of age, takes over the skateboard, executing neat double turns with no difficulty – to the admiration of the others. Stephen never smiles. But Andrew Hill grins his characteristic half-ashamed grin – pleased to be accepted by the older boys, to be part of the group.

When Stephen gets tired of the board and asks him to play football, his pleasure is complete. Stephen jigs the ball from his foot to his knee, to his other knee, and back to his foot, copying his heroes of the Liverpool team, then shouts 'Here, Andrew! Take it, Andrew,' kicking the ball to the much clumsier Andrew Hill – who just manages to return it. Eventually they have to ask a passerby the time, and, discovering it is eight o'clock, scatter in their different directions.

In school the next day Mrs Quin tells them that she will have to make out record cards for them all, before they go up to the juniors next year. The children cluster round her, some of them looking apprehensive. 'Why do you have to do them, Mrs Quin?' asked Leila Picken.

'So that the teachers in the juniors know what you've been doing – so they know what to expect of you.'

'Will it be hard?' asked Andrew.

'Well, hard-er,' replies his teacher, in her most reassuring voice. He looks unconvinced, and stares into space whilst Finn and Paul kick each other under the table. On the wall behind them Mrs Quin has pinned up a large sheet of paper. 'Here are some words to help you with your news and stories:

yesterday	today	tomorrow
last night	this morning	next week
last month	next month	next year
	a long time ago	

once upon a time

one day

Andrew's headmaster, Mr McCroskery, believes that it is possible to separate a child's life into very distinct stages. This is what he has observed during decades of teaching: 'At the infants stage the children are still much nicer. That is – between five and seven. After that, they become much more obtuse, and cunning, and aware. They really start to grow up at nine, it is the magical age at which they will change. Before that, between five and, well, eight really – you still have the wonderment, the receptiveness, the imagination. Between five and eight is a good stage. But between eight and twelve they start to be aware of environment and expectations. They become cynical – as much for their own protection as anything.'

Andrew's bedroom contains modern bedroom furniture, a single bed covered by a turquoise candlewick bedspread, and a large drawings of dinosaurs sellotaped to the walls – Andrew's own careful work. At frequent intervals the 81 bus grinds to a halt outside his window.

Andrew sat up in bed reading an Enid Blyton story. It was called *The Enchanted Wood*, an old-fashioned tale of magic lands, which he loved. Two or three chapters a night isn't enough – he will persuade any adult he can get hold of to read him Blyton's laboured prose until he rubs his own eyes, fighting sleep: 'I'd like to write books. I write in me diary – things like what I do, people's birthdays. If you tell me your birthday I'll put it in. In school I like writing stories, not news, because stories are good. Not much happens to me, really. Except sometimes I see ghosts. And I like my secrets. They're good. I don't tell mum and dad me secrets. Once I got a seed – with wings on – and planted it in a pot and watered it and it grew. Mum took it over to the parkie and he was going to plant it.' His face looks sad. 'But I don't know where it is. But mum said she'll ask the parkie and then I can go and see it and watch it grow. But I won't tell anybody in case the other boys find it and pull it up.

'When I'm by meself I like going in the park and doing secret things. I spy on people. Once I saw a man kicking down a fence. You're not allowed to do that. I watched him, and then I ran away. And once I found a tunnel – a real tunnel – somewhere in the park I'd never been before, and I went down it by meself. But after that

Andrew Lewis said he'd seen it, too, and he'd been there, and he'd seen the *real Devil* in it. So I didn't go down there again. I find tunnels and holes in trees and things like that — but I don't tell anybody. . . .' He looks up sharply. 'Why should I tell you all me secrets?

'I want two things. I want to be an artist; and I want Johnny to come. He's me cousin. When he comes we sleep in the spare room, and the ghost doesn't come because there's two of us — and we read and talk *all night*! I like Johnny better than anyone else in the world. He's a year older than me. He's coming down here in the summer holidays. . . . Oooh, I'm *dying* for the summer holidays.' For a second Andrew looks as though he could cry with the longing. 'I miss him. I tell him all me secrets. When he's been to stay here, I go back there to his house. Once we was in the park, me and Johnny and there was these little girls playing ball. And we broke up the game and took their ball. But they got their family who was somewhere else in the park, and they had *two dogs* — and they all ran after us. We was being chased by all these little girls and the two dogs! We had to leave the ball. But it wasn't fair. Fancy getting all that help and the dogs too, just for me and Johnny. . . . If I was the Incredible Hulk I'd have gone green and chased them right out of the park. I'd have roared at them with me eyes all red. That would be good. . . . But why *does* he change back all the time? And at the end of the programme, when he walks off by himself there's always that funny sad music. Why is the music sad?'

6 David

'It's like this: lesson, lesson, break; lesson, lunch, detention read out, then lesson, then rest, games, then detention at half past four. Then free time, till tea. On Wednesday we have sweets after lunch. If your parents don't know the sweet rule and send you some, you put them in your table box and they get passed round. They halve Mars bars and put them in the tin. We have five sweets when we've got the tables cleared. On Sundays we queue up for them. Tea is at six. We have ravioli, and bread and butter and jam, and things like that. It's finished at half past six, and then we play until a junior bell goes at a quarter to seven, and there's an outside bell for middles at ten past seven. Then the seniors at forty minutes past seven. When the bell goes we go on parade. When I hear the bell on Tuesday I normally rush, absolutely rush, and quickly get my socks up, because nearly everyone doesn't remember that it's sock day. Well, you take your socks upstairs and you pin them on the end of your bed and the matrons come round and wash them. And we have clean ones the next day. When we've gone up we quickly get undressed, and then we can play about. Normally we play with Dudhia's sponge — sometimes 'skimmer' and sometimes football. When we get into bed we read or talk, or do codes. Lights out is at half past seven. Normally Nicholls — he's our dorm leader — says, 'Turn the lights out, Watson,' because Watson's bed is nearest the door. When the lights are out we carry on talking a titchy bit, or we do finger language, like this. . . .'

David delights in describing his school routine. He is eight years old, and a boarder at St Edmund's, a prep school near Hindhead in Surrey. The days are portioned out by bells, the minutes watched by rules. David knows the rules, understands and accepts the rewards and punishments. The good ones will strive to attain quarter-stars, half-stars and full stars. The naughty ones do not know what happens when you reach a whole star — for them it is 'stripes' 'changebacks', detentions, and even a whack with a gym shoe: 'When I'm at school and I've done something I know whether it's right or wrong. I get into trouble for things like . . . er . . . running about in the dorm, talking after lights out, and. . . . Well, when you get a stripe you have to have some punishment from your division leader for having the stripe. Stoney Major is going to be our division leader next term. So he says, Do five changebacks. Then you have to get into your blue and white rugger vest, shorts, blue jersey, socks and boots, and change back again, and you do it five times. It's so you don't get free time.

'You see, you add ten points for your division if you get a star, and minus ten points if you get a stripe. If you are in any matches, first eleven, or second eleven, it's two points. If you are in athletics against another school, I think you get five points, and if you win a race you get an extra five points. At the end of the year if your division wins, the division leader gets a shield with all the names on it of the division leaders who have got it. . . . That's why they punish you for a stripe with changebacks. If you do something wrong after lights out, like I pushed my trunk one night under the bed and it made a noise . . . then I got sent to Mr Bennett and he gave me a whack with a gym shoe with my dressing gown still on. I had to bend over a chair, make my nose touch the seat and my hands touch my toes. Then go back to bed. I get that about once a week! No – about five times in the whole term. I was quite good in my first term. I got two stripes and two stars. On my second one I got two stripes and two stars. On my third term . . . well, six stripes.'

The same school rules have existed for years; and even now the fathers of boys presently at the school remember them. The smell too is the same: a mixture of old wood, polish, chalk, and boys' clothing; whilst the stuffed grizzly bear in the hall still stalks into the dreams of the timid newcomer who has cried himself to sleep in the snuffling dormitory. St Edmund's school moved from Norfolk to the present site in 1900 – a cluster of red-brown brick buildings standing in about 30 acres of leafy grounds. There are well-kept playing fields, a golf course and a sheltered open-air swimming pool with diving boards and a slide. But St Edmund's does not present any air of opulence: its dormitories and classrooms are simple with an air of functional shabbiness as ingrained as the initials long carved into the old-fashioned wooden desks.

David started as a day boy three months before he was seven. He boarded for two weeks during his fifth term while his parents went on holiday, then started after Christmas as a boarder proper. At first he missed home, although he hid his feelings well. 'In our dorm, one new boy cried first night, second night, third night, fourth night. I felt sorry for him. I only felt homesick on the sixth day. I don't know why. I was trying to go to sleep and I couldn't, so I thought of mummy. And I cried a bit then. And I forgot how many posters I had in my bedroom at home, so I couldn't make up a story about them. Normally when I'm in bed at home I look at the posters on the wall and think, Ah, Tomsk [he's a Womble], and I make up a story about him; or Paddington, oh yes, Paddington – let me see, Paddington and the obstacle race. So when I'm at school I try to remember them because I haven't got anything to make me go to sleep. . . . I thought I would like being a day boy better, because I could always go home, and get more things to eat, and go to bed late. So I didn't *really* want to board. But then I had to and I liked it. Well, I missed mummy and daddy and the farm. But I didn't know we'd get sweets on Sundays, and it was really fun in the dorm because we could talk, and fight, and play before we got into bed. 'It's really good because there's a mirror in the dorm, and I can look at it and see into the other mirror in the dorm which looks on to the door and see if matron's going past. You see, we have a club, a secret club. There's six of us from the dorm, and we call it the Spying Six because we spy on matron. Well, we crawl under the beds when she's talking to sister, and we hear what she's talking about. The whole dorm knows about it but they won't tell anybody. Anyway, we can't spy on anybody else. . . .

'In the dorm I would really like to be in Cowling's place, next to Nicholls. You see, the door is *here*, Nicholls is *here*, and Cowling is *here* – so you can see if there's going to be a raid or not. It's really funny then. We raided West (that's another dorm, near ours). We went round the corner and we stood behind the cupboard, and if you look through, there's a gap, and we can see if they're going out. When they went out, me and Cowling and Wallis went in and wrecked their beds. We didn't wreck Stoney Minor's because he's their dorm leader. And we have dorm fights. Normally Cowling and Rainer against me and Rice. We fight with teddies, and hard books, and Watson – he's the youngest person in the dorm – he has this snake with two eyes, and he slaps us with that. . . .'

There is no time for friendly fights in the morning. The day starts at about 7 a.m. with the inevitable bells – tumbling the boys from their beds, urging them to run to splash their faces under the taps in the large draughty bathroom. Then they race back and dress in their uniform of grey trousers, socks and blue airtex shirt – with some of them choosing a long-sleeved shirt and tie, even though it is supposed to be summer. They make their beds, pulling the brightly striped coverlets smooth, and arrange their teddy bears on top. All day, as the sun moves round the large light room, the animals wait: Snoopys, tigers, a furry lion, yellow bears; on David's bed, a strange, barely classifiable dark-brown creature with no ears.

Feet clatter down the wooden staircase, and the boys rush to their lines in the hall, under the gaze of the masters. When the lines are complete, and Headmaster Peter Weekes nods, a senior boy says, 'File into chapel,' watching that the lines are straight and no one talks. A slight scuffling; they pass from the high hall through a low dark passage into the school chapel, bowing their heads and quieting down as they make the transition. In the small, low-roofed building, warm with polished pews and deep-stained glass, they kneel in rows, whilst the masters take their seats in a row along the back. The chaplain, in black gown and clerical collar kneels to one side, leading the responses from *The Book of Common Prayer*, in the short but formal service. Even David and his friends hardly nudge and fidget. The collective voice of St Edmund's choruses loudly and with conviction:

> 'Then fancies flee away,
> I'll fear not what men say.
> I'll labour night and day,
> To *be* a pilgrim.'

When the service is over, at about five past eight, the boys file into the main school, and into the refectory for breakfast. There are long polished tables in gold-coloured wood under walls decorated with murals of kings, knights and saints, gleaming with gold detail. As the division heads dish out Weetabix, bowls clatter in a rising hubbub of noise. After the cereal, the boys wolf down baked beans, milk and toast, then rush out to play in the half hour before lessons begin at nine o'clock.

The school timetable is similar to that of any formal junior school, apart from the inclusion of subjects like French, Latin and history for even the youngest boys. But the atmosphere at St Edmund's is utterly different – the boys inhabit a far more structured world. Their homes may be in Singapore or Surrey; they may be Moslem and so miss chapel; their parents may be divorced, stable, rich or struggling slightly to meet the fees – whatever home may be like, school for the boarders shapes their vocabulary, their ideas, their mannerisms, their expectations. It is a small and private world-within-world – a well-defined system and hierarchy in which they know their place.

As the end of the summer term approached, there was a slackening in the air, a consciousness that nothing mattered very much except doing well for the school in cricket matches, or gaining points for your division in the school sports. Yet even at the beginning of the last week, lessons droned on as usual — the classrooms hot and sweaty, flies buzzing against the windows overlooking the tennis courts.

David's desk is second from the front in the third row, in the newish hut-like annexe. He is small for his age, slightly built but athletic, with a face which smiles readily, and a strange upper lip which tucks in for the smile to reveal his teeth. When he talks to an adult he has a habitual nervous gesture of raising the palm of his hand to his nose, then pulling it down as if he were perpetually swatting a troublesome fly.

Like all the others he leaps to his feet when Mr Ridett strides into the room, and chants *'Bon-jour Muhsewer.'* The French master turns, with a military air, to the blackboard and chalks: *'C'est lundi le dix juillet.'*

A piece of French prose is read out around the class, with Mr Ridett correcting the pronunciation. When it comes to David he mumbles in a monotone:

'Tante Marie et Oncle Maurice demeurent a Dinard. Dinard est une ville en Bretagne. Dinard est plus petit que Paris. . . .' — whilst one good French scholar in the class, a boy whose parents live in Switzerland, grins complacently at his execrable pronunciation.

Then, *'Davide,* what does *descendre* mean?' and, *'Davide, de quelle couleur est la vache?'*

'Brune.'

'Whole sentence, please.'

'Er . . . *le vache est brun.'*

'La vache — elle est brune. Repeat that, please, Davide.'

David wriggles in his seat. All he can think about is the Six Schools Athletics meeting that afternoon in which he will be running for the school. Each time he imagines taking his position at the start of a race his stomach gives a lurch and slips sideways. The French lesson; the subsequent tedious account of how Cromwell took an unfair advantage by training his Ironsides as hard fighting men, and gaining the support of 20,000 unpredictable Scots; and the hissing sibilants as his friends shoot up their hands to answer, pleading, 'Sir, oh, *sir'* — all of it seemed interminable and irrelevant.

Latin is even worse: the master's voice intones, *'cuncti in cauponam intrant. Caupo alios servos iubet canes detrahere, alios ad raedam mittit....'* But Mr Dalmon notes his mind is wandering and barks, 'Which group does *'servo'* belong to?'

David puts his hand over his nose. 'Er ... one, sir.'

'Yes. Now decline it for me.'

'Um, *servo, servare, servavi, servatum.* Er, no! *Servo, servas, servat, servamus, servatis, servant.'*

He looks up hopefully. Mr Dalmon just nodded, suppressing the faintest smile.

After lunch, the English master remarks to David, now changed into his track suit: 'You look like a bag of rags, laddie.' And the boy, who had been told to save his energy whilst the other boys shivered in the warm sun at the swimming pool, looks embarrassed and pale.

The Haslemere Preparatory Schools Athletics Meeting took place on the field of a local comprehensive school. The boys from Fernden, Highfield, St Edmund's, Edgeborough, Haslemere and Amesbury arrived in buses, dressed in their coloured track suits. Mothers pulled up in their Morrises and Renaults, and positioned folding chairs to watch as the games masters in saggy-bottomed track suits paced the field with a self-conscious roll, surrounded by clutches of worshipping boys. David, one of twenty-four boys representing St Edmund's, squatted under a tree with his friends, noting with mounting apprehension that his race, the Under 10 100 metres, would be the sixteenth event – with all those cricket balls thrown, hurdles leapt, shots putted and long jumps measured before he could work off the adrenalin.

When his mother arrived, a small shy woman with straight dark hair cut in a bob, wearing an Indian printed skirt and flat sandals, he greeted her with the laconic manner schoolboys adopt in front of their friends, unwilling to receive a kiss, twisting aside slightly from an embrace. Valerie goes to see most school matches, as their home is only a twenty-minute drive from the school: 'I wouldn't have been nearly so happy to send him boarding at this stage, far away. The thing that makes it bearable from my point of view is that he is so near and that I can go up to matches and see him. So in fact one doesn't lose contact. At all. I would hate it if we lived a long way away and I never saw him except at half term.'

She stood and watched the first fifteen events diligently, cheering,

'Come on, St Edmunds,' with the other mothers, and carefully marking down the results in her programme.

Next to her a father boomed, 'Well *done*, Deane, well *done*,' and heartily clapped his own winning son on the shoulder as if he were a stranger. But Valerie was growing more and more nervous as David's race approached. 'Oh, you *do* so want them to do well. It seems to matter so much to them,' she said, biting her lip. Then, as David stood waiting in his lane, third from the inside, her knuckles whitened on the fence: 'It's . . . he, he looks so much *smaller* than the others, doesn't he?'

There was a moment's silence, then, 'On your marks . . . get set. . . .' and the crack, as the six boys hurled themselves forward, arms pumping, hearts thumping – blue sky, green playing field, and the watching faces blurring to nothing as they ran and ran towards that white tape, stretching and straining towards . . . honour for the school? Points for their divisions? Or simply not being last? Whatever the goal, David's face was contorted into a grimace, his mother shouted, 'Come *on*, David, David, come *on*,' and he flashed past the winning post, close on the heels of two other boys.

Valerie let out a sigh-groan that was half pleasure and half disappointment: 'He came third. Well, third is perfectly all right. Third is quite a *respectable* place. I think he's done jolly well. *Jolly* well. I must go and find him. . . .' And she rushed off amongst the mothers, masters and boys to congratulate her son.

That night David lay in his bed in the dorm and thought about the race. He imagined winning. His relay team had been placed third, too, and St Edmund's had finally won third place in the total, beaten by Edgeborough and Haslemere. Third: it seemed an ordinary sort of position to get, neither excellent nor terrible, just rather ordinary. But at least he had been placed.

At last after the Latin play, the golf final, the French play, the school concert, the staff versus school cricket match, the chaos of packing, and the final prize giving – the trunks were stacked in front of the school and the cars started to arrive.

Valerie collected her son and drove him home to the postcard-pretty village of Thursley, ten miles from Guildford in Surrey, where they have lived since 1963. Thursley is no longer a 'proper' village community; most of the old cottages have been 'dollied up' (Valerie's phrase) and bought by commuters. The village is what David's father calls a 'half-and-half- – with half the population dashing off to London each morning, and the other half, retired, staying at home to prune the roses. The pride of the village is the 900-year-old church, with Saxon windows in the chancel, where David still sings in the choir, when he is home from school.

David's home is a sixteenth-century timbered cottage called 'Wheeler's Farm' which looks — with the roses round the door, the long straight path to the front porch, and the walled garden — exactly like the house a child might draw and colour, asked to portray the sort of picture-book home he would like most of all. Inside, there is a slight air of genteel dilapidation, and Valerie apologises profusely for its condition. The small sitting room is pretty with chintz and antiques, the dining room filled by an elegant oval table, but the kitchen is dark, with yellowing walls, a massive yellow-cream Aga oven around which flies hover ceaselessly, and old brown Formica units. Next to it is a drying room full of muddy wellingtons, ancient raincoats, the dog basket, and washing. John and Valerie spend as little as possible on their house. They own 20 acres of countryside — their three daughters have their ponies, and all their children go to the type of schools they approve.

The week David arrived home from school it was haymaking time. Gina and Emma, who are thirteen and fifteen, were home from St Mary's School, Calne, and Pippa, who is seventeen had finished her A-levels at the sixth-form college to which they had sent her after St Mary's. The weather stayed warm, and whilst the rest of his family did all the work, David rode around on the back of the cart in the sunshine, smelling the sweet smell of the cut grass, and glad to be wearing his old jeans once more. To the right of their house is a cobbled stable yard; beyond that the old barn which is warm and musty with hay, and the granary on its little stilts, in which David likes to hide.

His parents do not use their land, apart from grazing and providing hay for the horses. John is an accountant with a firm of metal brokers in the City and leaves the house each day at 7.30 a.m., drives to the station, catches his train, goes to his office and does not return home until about 7.30 at night.

John, who married Valerie when she was twenty and he was ten years older, clearly regrets that he has so little time at home, on his land: 'I should be fifteen years younger to work in the City. The strains are considerable. I make my own pressures in any case — I think we all do.'

Valerie added that just lately her husband had been feeling 'terribly tired'. They sat one evening in their sitting room, after David had gone to bed and whilst the three girls were washing up the dinner dishes, and talked about 'Taffy' (David's family nickname) and the education they had chosen for him. They said that they had chosen St Edmund's because they knew people who had sent their sons there, and they were impressed by Peter Weekes, the headmaster. There was never any question about the *type* of education he would receive.

Valerie: 'Our local primary school is in the next village. That's the one he would go to, or should go to. And it's absolutely enormous – forty or fifty to a class. And it's not – well, it doesn't have a good reputation. It's a huge village, and it takes people in from all around. It's not one of those nice little tiny village schools.'

John: 'But there are one or two in other villages dotted around.'

Valerie: 'Well, there are. . . .'

John: 'But we never really thought about sending them there.'

Valerie: 'We didn't. We found Mrs Frost at College Hill Kindergarten who was very good and very reasonable. She taught them their basic three Rs very well. They learned to read and write at the age of four and do sums, tables. They had a jolly good basic grounding. That type of education seems to suit our children better – the more traditional, formal type.'

John: 'You see, we made a big decision about twelve years ago and put down some money for their private education.'

Valerie: 'It doesn't anything like cover it.'

John: 'Well, we took out insurance which doesn't cover it – but we made the decision about twelve years ago when Pippa was five. The three girls were five, three and one, and Taffy wasn't even thought of. We put down what we thought in those days was a large capital sum, to cover the fees for six years.'

Valerie: 'Allowing a little for inflation.'

John: 'Unfortunately, the insurance companies in those days didn't build in a very big inflation factor, so in fact now we still get the money from the insurance, but gradually it gets less and less. So it only covers a third now.'

Valerie: 'At that stage, when fees were not as astronomical as they are now, we took it for granted that they would be educated privately.'

John: 'I think if we hadn't done so, the grandparents would have insisted on it.'

Valerie: 'I mean, we didn't ask, Are we going to send the children to state school? We didn't debate that aspect of it – we rather assumed.'

John: 'And somehow, we managed to keep going.'

Valerie: 'I'm sure people don't realize what a sacrifice it is to send your children to private schools. They say you're buying privilege, and that sort of thing. They should realize in fact that it's a great struggle to do it — after all, we are paying rates and tax, we are making our contribution towards the money that goes into state education. And at the same time one is paying for one's children's education. But we do it because we think it's. . . .'

John: 'We think it's the *best*. But in my view it would be no good sending them to the private sector just for the sake of doing so, because I think some of the state schools would be better than a lot of private schools. If we are going into the private sector then we've got to go for the best schools. There's no good doing it otherwise. In other words, if he couldn't pass from St Edmund's into Marlborough, which was my school, then I'd have serious thoughts about what to do.'

Valerie: 'We certainly wouldn't send him to a second-rate boys' school.'

John: 'But if he's not that academic he might like to take up some career where an academic background isn't required.'

Valerie: 'But at St Edmund's they seem to have a pretty good success rate. Most of the boys go to the public schools they want to. Quite a few of them get scholarships or exhibitions. . . .'

(BM: You used the phrase, 'buying privilege'. What is the privilege you are buying?)

John: 'Well, it's something that nobody can take from you. It's difficult to define, but if you haven't got it, you are lacking something. If you *have* got it, that's fine.'

Valerie: 'No, the way I look at it — it's smaller classes, much more individual attention. An academic atmosphere, too. I mean, frankly, I can't think how the poor teachers manage to teach anything in state schools with the enormous classes. I think they are wonderful people, but. . . .'

John: 'And you can do things and take up interests which you might not study again, but which you've got. . . .'

Valerie: 'The facilities are there.'

John: 'Yes. I think too that if a big school has a good name, you go along on the crest of a wave in many ways. Tradition.'

Valerie: 'It is just the general atmosphere and the way they influence each other. Discipline is good, and the day is so organized, there is no time for boredom.'

Denise

Mandy

Gemma

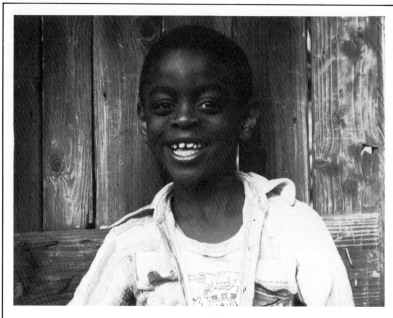

Donald

Andrew

David

Keith

Moya and Co.

Melanie

Rajesh

Wendy

Douglas

(BM: When David first boarded, even though the girls were already boarding, was it a shock?)

Valerie: 'Yes, it was. I was surprised how much I missed him.'

John: 'You were very upset, weren't you?'

Valerie: 'Yes, I was terribly upset to start with. I knew he was enjoying it, and it was rather silly because I'd been looking forward to it. I was thinking how nice and peaceful it would be. But then, it just hit me. I don't know. He's not a great letter writer, and in any case they only write letters on Sundays and not in between time, and so you didn't hear anything. And when he did write he didn't say much.'

John: 'Well, actually as term went on you saw a lot of him because he was in matches.'

Valerie: 'Yes. The first time was after two and a half weeks, and after that I felt fine. It was just when I didn't really know how he was. I was sure that if there had been anything wrong they would have rung up – but it seemed silly for me to ring up and say, How is he? I think the chief thing he gets is companionship, which he doesn't have at home.'

John: 'You see, with the girls – there's a five-year gap between him and Gina, so he's very much the little brother. Then the boy across the way is boarding as well. Anyway, David is a very independent character.'

Valerie: 'I think they are far more part of the place when they are boarding. It tends to make children more independent of their parents. There's far more "belonging". And he's very confident. And bright, although his school report wasn't very impressive, and he thinks too much about games.'

John: 'I certainly would like David to do well academically and do all the things – well, I think every father thinks this – do all the things I've failed to do in life. I suppose that's why one has children in some ways.'

Valerie: 'I don't think it ought to be.'

John: 'Well, I think if you haven't had any startling success in life, you do rather want your children to.'

The family did not go away for a summer holiday. Only Emma went to stay with a school friend in Cyprus; the others spent the long holiday at home. Mornings would dawn brightly. David would leap out of bed, with its pink candlewick bedspread, dress quickly, and knock a tennis ball around the walls of his bare little bedroom – avoiding his precious posters. After his bowl of cereal he would look out at the weather – usually noting the billowing clouds that almost invariably crowded the horizon by ten o'clock. Too often rain would follow.

If the weather stayed fine, he would play alone with the tennis ball and racquet, threatening the front windows of the house. Or wander out into the stable yard where Pippa, Emma and Gina were mucking out their horses, Flint, Saffron, and Shah, or cleaning their tack. He would ride his bicycle through the village streets – until after repeated warnings his mother met him once again riding with no hands, and confiscated it. Or wander aimlessly across the field, thinking about his games of chess with Gina, or with his father, who taught him at the age of five. Moves. Tactics. How he could have won. How Gina gets more furious as his game improves. How he could have taken his father's queen. . . .

Though he did not mind playing alone, when he chose he could call on Oliver, Marcus, Andrew and Simon, who lived in the village, and were also home from their schools. The four boys would play hide-and-seek in the bracken behind Marcus's house, or in the warm and rustling barn at Wheeler's Farm. Or french cricket, or team games – frustrating only because of the smallness of the teams. Even in the summer drizzle they could wander in their wellingtons and anoraks, excited by the prospect of a storm, watching the bracken soften and drip, diverting slugs with sticks; or shelter in the dry patch under a tree, listening to the patter overhead.

David's sisters would grow irritated with him five or six times a day, chorusing: 'Oh, don't be so *silly*, Taffy!' when he had an inexplicable fit of giggles, or made a silly joke, or tried to persuade his mother to send away for an offer from the back of a cereal packet. 'Don't be so *silly*, Taffy,' affected him not at all. His mother would, if she felt he was being unfairly persecuted, defend him from his sisters; and in any case, he decided privately that girls were pretty feeble. His sisters were the only ones he could remotely tolerate, but even they seemed bad-tempered, and uninterested in things like hide-and-seek in the bracken, and football, and golf. David had little interest in their horses.

'If I didn't have my sisters I'd have no one to play Monopoly and chess with me. But if I had three brothers, that would be fantastic. Because they would probably all go to St Edmund's and we could play football on Sundays. My sisters think I'm a nuisance. But I don't know I am.'

Most of all he enjoyed the weekends, when his father was home. They would drive together to Hankley Golf Course, where David is already a junior member, and try to improve his game: 'Actually I'm quite good. Last week he gave me three on the first hole and two on the rest, and it worked out like this – three handicap: first hole nine for me, six for daddy. Then six – five, eight – five, five – five, seven – seven. I easily beat him by four – five. Six – seven and five – four, eight – six and nine – six. I think it was like that. Don't you know what that all means?' He looks impatient and slightly pitying. 'You see, I've won, counting the first one which daddy won, er . . . one, two, three, four . . . EIGHT! I won eight, daddy won two, I think. I nearly always win. Daddy should give me only one – handicap, that is . . . I like being with daddy. We sometimes quarrel, but only about once a year. Mummy gets the worst from daddy by dropping cups and things. She's *always* doing that.'

David looked forward to the holiday when he was at school; he looked forward to the new term when he was at home. He said that he liked home and school the same. But next term he would have to work harder and think less about games: 'Daddy said so. My report this term was sort of medium – some good, some bad. There's something like twelve subjects and I got about seven bad, and five all right. After St Edmund's I'm going to Marlborough. I hope. Then Cambridge. Daddy went to Marlborough and Cambridge. But he didn't go to St Edmund's. I think I'll have to work very hard at Marlborough. You see there was an Oxford exam paper which Mr Caldwell – he's the history master – showed us. A history exam paper. Out of twenty questions we could hardly answer two of them. But I've got, let me see, nine years to learn all that – if I go at seventeen. If I go. I don't know what I'd *do*. I'd have to look in my report and see which is the best thing . . . Latin, I think.

'Mummy and daddy and I went to Marlborough, so I've seen it. We walked around. I've seen the different houses: A house, B house, C house, I think it is. The school looked nice. But I don't know what penalties they have . . .

'I like living in the country, but I'd like to go up to London and come home each day, like daddy does. Or perhaps I could be a farmer. Of course, I've *got* to go to Cambridge, if I pass. Anyway, daddy does both.'

BM: But this isn't a real farm.)

'We are going to get bullocks, because we've got a lot of hay. We've got four horses and two dogs. We used to have a cat. So it's nearly a farm. It would be nice to be a farmworker, I think.'

(BM: Do you know the difference between a farmer and a farm-worker?)

'I'd say . . . because if you are a farmer you just live on a farm and own it, and you tell your workers what to do. And when you work, you have to . . . let's say, clean out the pig sty. So I'd rather be a farm-*er*. Except that I wouldn't mind being a farmworker if it just meant putting out the horses. I like horses. I don't like pigs!'

David receives eight pence each week as pocket money, one penny for each year of his life. During term-time, Valerie saves it up for him to spend on 'leave-outs' — when twice a term she can collect him at 2 p.m. on Saturday and have him home until Sunday evening.

'When I was five I got five p. When I'm a hundred years old I'll get one pound.' He grins. 'But my mother won't be around then, so I won't. I'll be in my home opening my thing from the Queen. Telegram, yes. Congratulating me. I don't mind the idea of being a hundred. I might be old and wrinkled, but I'll still be able to play cricket. When I'm sixty I will. I've got to keep energetic. I've got to keep on running down to the shop for mummy. When I'm older I'll go seven miles a day, jogging or sprinting. I've *got* to keep energetic. Why? Well, *I* just think I have.'

Autumn

7 Keith

Penarth is the posh end of Cardiff, where solid brick-built Victorian houses, sitting securely in walled and leafy gardens, overlook the wide mouth of the Severn. Sleek fibreglass sailing dinghies lie above the pebble beach, nylon-wrapped – to be wheeled down to the water on Sundays by young men seizing the end of the sailing summer. Down on the beach boys skim stones into the surf, watched by the parents of stumbling toddlers, who point and exclaim. The pier is a fantasy concoction of bright sea-green paint and frilly white wrought iron, pegged to the sea by a hundred taut fishing lines.

Keith Davies used to fish there. He would take the twenty-minute walk from Cogan (the less affluent area where he lives) into Penarth itself, carrying his brown fishing bag, and fantasizing about the bites he would get. But his older brother Peter broke his fishing rod – accidentally Peter says, deliberately Keith says – and so now all Keith can do is watch enviously. If the walk to the pier seems too long, he can wander to Penarth Docks, nearer his home, and, standing on a pile of rubbish, watch the grey windswept water. The fish bite even better there, he says. He stares at the rows of moored boats: small cruisers, fishing boats, and sailing boats with the wind pinging their masts. Keith, the keen fisherman, has been on a boat once. It was a wooden motor boat on a pond in a park, and his stepfather was steering.

But that was a few years ago. Keith is ten now, and his stepfather is in prison again. For the last six years he has grown up to the sounds of breaking furniture, shouts, and his mother's screams. He has seen her bruises and black eyes the morning after, and become accustomed to the clenching of his stomach when the angry shouts start once more downstairs. When his stepfather is in prison, the family waits for him to be released and come looking for them once more. Then Keith's mother's nerves grow frayed, and she takes it out on Peter, eleven, Keith, Darren, five, and four-year-old Debbie.

Keith spends the time he is not at school roaming the streets with his friends, or quarrelling with his mother. They cannot speak to each other without shouting. Marion Griffiths, a small, dark-haired woman of thirty two, admits that she cannot get on with this son, although her life has been such that to scream at and slap all the children is natural to her. But Keith is the most like her – he shares her looks and mannerisms.

Marion will sit laughing and talking, until Keith walks into the room, and then she seems to wait for trouble. Keith will stroll along the road with a friend, grinning and sharing a secret, until he walks into the room where his mother sits smoking in her corner, and then his face will close. Keith Davies' life, as he starts back in September for his last year at primary school, is a struggle. His mother understands, though she is too locked into the fortress of her own fear to help. 'As soon as *he* gets out this time, he'll come looking for us. . . .' When Marion sits in the sitting room of her small council house, and talks about her two marriages, she is describing Keith's life, too – all he has known. For Keith is silent and will not talk.

Marion Griffiths: 'I was born in Wales in 1946, but my mother's Irish – from Belfast. For years my dad was a casemaker, up in the quarry. I was fifteen when I left school, and worked in a shop for eleven months. Then I left home and went to work in a factory in Brynmawr; when I was seventeen I went away to work in the Isle of Man. It was when I came back from there that I met my first husband. I didn't have to get married, like. I met my husband, Dai Davies he was called, through a friend. He worked in the pits. The banns went out on my nineteenth birthday, and I was married four weeks to the day from the day I met him. And as I say, we didn't have to get married. It was a bit quick to have known that, even if I had! I came out of hospital with Peter on my twentieth birthday.

'Dai was killed in a car crash. We were married six years. He'd missed the last bus, and these boys that he knew were in the pub, and one of them was driving. There was three of them in the van, and it was the driver that caused the accident. On a straight road he had overtook, and he couldn't get back in, and the oncoming traffic. . . . There was some bad injuries and that, but Dai was the only one that got killed. Oh, it was terrible. I was shocked. . . .

'I was still in shock when I remarried, 'cos I remarried after six months. Met and married in six months. Davey's brother, Alan Griffiths, was a friend of my first husband's, and his wife Diane said, Come out with us, like. We were in this pub in Caerphilly and he was there, Davey, and I liked him. I thought he was a good-looking boy; I fancied him and everything. He was twenty-seven – he's two years older than me. So we got married. Mind, I was told what he was like before, but you don't see that. By his sister-in-law, Diane.

It was his drinking. His mother thought he would never get married. . . .

'So we got married. I left him six months after we was married, when I had just caught for Darren. I'd had the coil fitted after I'd had Keith but he kept on and on; and I wondered if it would be different if he had. . . . You know, he didn't have much. He was good with Peter and Keith, mind. Yes, very good. So I thought, like, it's only natural he wants one of his own, ain't it? I thought he would be different. So I went – I was scared stiff to go and have the coil took out 'cos I didn't like it much when I had it put in. So I caught straight away for Darren.

'Oh, he'd already started then, Davey-boy. How can I explain to you? My worst fear was of what he was going to do to me, you see, the threats and everything. I've had plenty of bumps, but never a good hammering until I left him two years ago – you know what I mean? That was when he stood down at me as if I was a punch bag. Oh, he's tried to strangle me . . . but I've always got away, you know what I mean? I've had the kicks and punches but he's never held me there long enough. He's always been drinking so I've always been able to run faster than him. He's come after me a few times but never caught me.

'Anyway, I left him after six months. I took Peter and Keith to my mother's and we stayed there. I had to go in for a separation, a legal separation. So six months after I'd left him I finally goes to court. I'd seen a solicitor and everything. So I goes to court in Woodchurch – it's a small place between Cardiff and where I used to live, Caerphilly – and my solicitor never turns up. The court hadn't been informed or anything. So they rung my solicitor's office, and she had been taken sick, but they hadn't even bothered to send a replacement or anything. So it was adjourned.

'*He* was there. I dunno who came out first, but we went different ways. So I thought, I'll go in the café and have a cup of tea across the road from where the bus stop was. I goes over there . . . and he came in then, asked if he could sit down, got talking . . . and I went bloody back to him, didn't I?'

Four-year-old Debbie was playing round Marion's feet with a mutilated dolly, and when Darren, her five-year-old brother, came home from school, they both disappeared into the back garden. Marion's small council house backs on to a playing field, where the children can run wild, and she counts herself lucky that she does not live in a flat. 'I used to have more than this, I used to have a real home with nice stuff in it. But he sold the lot. Smashed a lot too. He

sold the two single beds the kids were sleeping in. Nice fridge. . . .
I didn't have a posh home, I had a nice home. Sold the bloody lot.
'Till I ended with a house full of junk.'

Upstairs there are three small bedrooms; downstrairs, a sitting
room, kitchen and bathroom. Marion has not lived there long and
does not know how long she will stay. When Davey comes out of
prison he finds out where they have moved to, or terrorizes a neighbour into telling him. Then he comes. So Marion applies for council
transfers in fear – even though she and her husband are now
divorced, and even though there is a court injunction for him not to
molest her.

Keith rapped at the front door first, and lurched into the room
red-faced and panting. He is fair-skinned, with reddish hair and his
mother's sharp features – a contrast to his older brother Peter,
round-faced and gentle, who strolled into the house next. It was the
first day of the autumn term; Keith had returned to Cogan Primary
School for his last year.

Peter had started at the comprehensive school in Penarth. He
wore his new black trousers, grey pullover and striped tie – and was
very pleased with himself. 'It's great. We start proper work next
week. This week we're just looking. We got some books but not all
of them. Look, mam, this is what we'll be doing.' A grubby piece of
paper – his timetable.

Then he handed his free school meal tickets to Marion, who
looked worried: 'What do we do with them? I'll have to tear one off
each day and give it you. What happens if I forget? What happens if
you lose it?'

Keith chipped in crossly: 'He gets nuthin'.'

Marion was not listening: 'Or if I lose the whole lot? Now where
can I put them in this mess?'

Keith was kicking the side of the vinyl armchair. 'When will I go
to his school?'

'Oh, you know. Next September!' replied Marion impatiently.

Keith groaned: 'That means there's a whole year to wait. A whole
year.'

When he had stumped upstairs Marion explained that Keith and
Peter had always been together, and now Keith felt left behind
because Peter had moved up. 'I'm having a lot of problems with him
now, like. Sometimes I could kill him. He won't do as he's told.
Pete's much better. He's more like his dad was – easy going.'

A little later, when Keith's friend came to the door to ask if he
could go to the swimming baths, there was a minor scene. Keith

looked sullen, whilst Marion expostulated: 'Keith – you *know* there's no money. I gave you all money for sweets yesterday, so now there's no money for you to go to the baths. So *don't ask!*' Keith's face grew redder, and he left the house.

That night, after all four kids had gone to bed, Marion sat watching television until closedown. Then she too went to bed. But she could not sleep. The cough kept her awake, and when awake she brooded: 'I listen to every little creak and I think it's him coming for me again. It's my nerves.'

Marion: 'I stayed, then I left again – I don't remember now 'cos I left so many times and went back. You know, you stick it for as long as you can. When I went back to him the first time he was good as gold for a few weeks. He would go without the drink – because there was no way he could be any different in the drink. He always said that I'd never had no reason for leaving. No cause, no reason, and he thought he was the perfect man, like! Never worked or anything – never mind that! Anyway I did go back . . . . I just honestly thought then that he'd change. But he was too old to change, you know. Even when we first got married I should have known it, but they say love is blind, and it was sort of on the rebound from . . . from *that*. I never really thought about Dai. . . . I hadn't forgotten him but I dunno what I had to gain. But when I used to live in fear of *him* and everything, I used to think, "Dai bloody died and left me." You know what I mean? I used to feel evil towards him for dying. For leaving me to . . . meet *him*. 'Cos as far as I know we would have still been together, ain't it?

'Davey had been in prison before I met him, but the first time he went in after we was married was when I was pregnant with Debbie. That was an accident. The only one that was planned was Darren. I'd gone back, and left him again. He used to drink continuous then, and he'd got into trouble in a pub and put a glass in some fella's face. Then I went back to him, 'cos it took a long time to get to court, and I caught for Debbie. He was given three years in Dartmoor. Well, of course I thought, now was the chance – if he was gonna change it would be now. I used to go and visit him every month, in Dartmoor, carrying the pushchair, with Peter and Keith carrying bags for me. I had to take clothes. All I could take for me was a change of underwear 'cos I couldn't carry the nappies. He didn't do three years – worse luck, now I know now what happened. He was a good prisoner and he got parole so he only did one year.

'I had these dreams that he'd be different. But the day he came out, as soon as I seen him I could tell he'd been drinking. Twelve o'clock the train arrived in Cardiff, and he'd been drinking. Oh, that was the finish then, you know.

'I stuck it for a month – left him a month after he'd come out of prison. I went into bed and breakfast, and then into Routh Camp. It was for homeless people. Bloody horrible – like a concentration camp. They put me in there. Debbie came down with, like dysentery – only it wasn't. A sickness. She was only a baby. Because the place, don't matter how clean you try to be, it wasn't very clean. And I had Darren and Keith and Peter and all. So I thought, I'm lost. I phoned my social worker, and told him I couldn't stick it. So I went back to Davey. He hadn't asked me this time – it was the only time I went back without him asking me.

'It wasn't long after that that I wanted to leave again. So I went to the social services in Caerphilly, and explained everything, and they said they'd see if they could get me into Routh Camp! I said, no way am I going into Routh Camp. The kids can go into care and I'll find something for myself. I said, I'm not going back. So they phoned around and told me about the refuge – for battered women in Cardiff. I took the kids there. Debbie was ten months old – Keith and Peter kept missing school and all. Mind, I'd never classed myself as a battered wife. I've seen women that look like a boxer coming out of a ring – you know, their faces. And to me *that* was battered. I hadn't been battered. Oh, I had plenty of bruises – all the different things he done, but never *really* beaten. I'd always lived in fear because of what he was going to do, as I said. He was telling me what he was gonna do to me – well, that alone was driving me scatty in the end. The different ways he was gonna kill me.

'It played on the kids' nerves, too – Keith's and Pete's. It must have. It was hurting them to be there, though he never laid a finger on them. But they just lived listening and waiting, and listening and waiting is worse than having a bloody good hiding, I tell you. I kept going back 'cos I'd nowhere to take them – and the refuge was ... well, it's a house full of women and children and that's not good for them either. But if he'd done what he did to me, in the beginning, then I don't think I ever would have gone back. Because I never went back after that.

'That night it happened he'd gone out and come in about two in the morning. Course he was drunk, stumbling about, and I could see by his face he was vicious. I didn't say nothing – daren't say nothing to him. I sat. . . . I'm ready to run. I was always ready to run. I sat on the chair by the door with my bag, 'cos when I used to run, I'd have no fags and no money for the phone, ain't it? This night I was prepared. I even had a fag in my bra, in case I couldn't grab the bag! Next thing I know, me and me bag and the chair ended up the back end of the room. I don't know what happened. From then on . . . oh, I was screaming. I tried my best to shelter the blows, ain't it? He'd . . . something had snapped in him and that's the gospel truth, and he was like a raving lunatic. All he done was punched − went for my head and my face. Everything got smashed, even the fireguard, even Debbie's little chair − bent so's you couldn't recognize it. I managed to get the back door open and fell outside, but was dragged back. I was punched till I couldn't scream any more. My voice had gone − I should have passed out. All I remember was lying there, and he's kneeling over me, and he's got his big fist drawn back for the final punch, and he's saying something. I can't hear him 'cos I'm punched to a jelly, like. He looks at me − then his grip goes off me, and I tries to slide away.

'I got out and I ran down the road − my legs was like jelly and I was ready to pass out. I was covered in blood, and that. I went to his father's who lived down the road and he said, Oh, my God, what's he done to her? The next day my mother seen me and she took me to hospital. You know when you see these cartoons and the bumps come right up on their heads − so you can see them? That's what my head was like.' She throws back her head and laughs. 'Oh, I've laughed about it since. If I was bald you'd have seen them all − these cartoon bumps! The hand I'd tried to shield myself with took a lot of blows and it was all black and yellow; I cried − I put a wet cloth round it. I couldn't open my mouth to eat. The doctor at the hospital said, He's made a pretty good job of it. And he turned to the nurse and said, This is the first one − this is the start of it. Once one comes in they all come in. He was talking about the summer evenings, you know − the drinking, the summer life. He asked if I wanted medical evidence for police proceedings, but I said, No, for divorce proceedings.

'I'll tell you what I think now − what about the kids? I remember them screaming, you know. Even through the noise and the punching I could hear them. And people around heard all this − they must have heard them kids. And nobody came. If it was only for the kids' sake! They didn't know whether the kids were being hit. People that knew me knew that he never touched the kids − but who would know, with them all screaming like that? But nobody phoned − nobody.'

It was sunny and very windy. Keith rushed home from school on Thursday and immediately changed into his football gear for school team practice on the field behind his house. Putting his boots on he called, 'Mum, I need new studs. The screw-in ones. In fact, I really need new boots.' From the kitchen Marion gave a derisive groan. Keith's expression did not change as he tied the laces: 'They're sixty pence a dozen.'

'Oh, that's not too bad.'

'And I really only need six.' He ran from the room, out of the house, and round the back to the field – dressed in his baggy white shorts and red football jersey. Marion watched him from the kitchen window, running to join the other boys who were dribbling foot-balls around.

'They never stop asking for things. Oooh, it gets me. Sometimes I don't know what I'm going to do with Keith. It's partly my fault, I know – Keith and Peter being like they are – though Peter's not as bad. It's my fault . . . I don't stand and talk to them about it, or anything. They come and tell me things and I'm not listening; my mind's full of everything and I say, Go away, I don't want to hear.

'I couldn't even talk to them when their father got killed. The husband of a friend of mine told them. He took them upstairs to his boy's bedroom and then he told them. And he said Peter was sitting taking it all in – listening, like. But Keith turned his back and was playing with this toy car, wheeling it backwards and forwards, backwards and forwards. Not even as if it was going in one ear and out the other, but as if it wasn't going anywhere at all. But I think now that it was going right in. Peter seemed to be listening, but he's happy-go-lucky, like his father was. But Keith. . . . Anyway, I've never talked to them about it. They never mentioned it again. They were only five and four years old when he died.

'When they both started school, one of them – I think it was Keith – came in crying one day. The kids had said, Your father's dead and buried in a box. Of course, they'd been told that he'd gone to heaven, not buried in the ground, ain't it? So I said, Just take no notice of them. He's gone to heaven; he's with Jesus. So they were all right. Their nan took them down to see Dai's grave, though. . . . Sometimes I feel sorry for them.'

When Keith came back from his football practice he asked if he could go to the baths. Marion became angry, because she had told him that they were all going out to visit the organizer of Welsh Women's Aid – a friend of Marion's – for a meal. 'I don't want to go,' he muttered, determined.

'Well, you've *got* to go. Don't push me, Keith, don't *do* it,' shouted Marion harshly.

The boy rushed upstairs in tears and refused to come down when she called. Marion grew tenser and tenser. 'What do I do? Just batter him? I do – but I don't think it does any good. But if I let him get his own way after I've told him, he'll just get worse and worse. So what do I do? This is where he needs a father – he needs a father's hand. But sometimes I could *kill* him, I really could. What do I do?'

Keith sat at the top of the stairs, his face streaked with sweat, dirt and tears. He picked furiously at imaginary specks of fluff on the patterned carpet, and mumbled in a tight little voice: 'I want to stay here on my own. I don't want to go out. I don't want to do anything. . . . It's not fair. I don't even get pocket money. All the others do. They get a pound a week. I never have anything like they do. She doesn't like me. She's always hitting me . . . because I won't go up the shop when she asks me. But I could be doing something, like watching a film on telly, and it's in the middle and I don't want to miss the end, so I say I'll go when it's finished. So she hits me, she does. She don't like me – and Peter don't like me. He snapped my fishing rod. He did. I threw a brick at him. I don't care if it would have killed him because he did it on purpose.'

Marion: 'Keith and Peter liked Davey at first. He could be quite good to them. People liked him without the drink. Nobody didn't want to know him in drink. It was like a split personality. I think without drink he'd have been different, 'cos whatever he put his hand to he could do – he could decorate, and he could paint – proper paintings, I mean. Nice paintings. It was a waste. That's why I used to feel sorry for him. He passed a test to do art at a college or something. But that was when he was young. And he started going with men much older than himself, and opted out of all that, and started drinking. Well, Davey joined the army when he was eighteen and he took up boxing and used to box for the army. It was only to prove to his father, I think. A lot of what's wrong with Davey, I think, is from his childhood. His dad used to beat his mother – she had a hell of a life.

'Since we've been divorced, well, since about '76, he's been in and out of prison. He's had about eighteen days' freedom in all that time, between all the little sentences. He's always good when he's in there, so's he gets remission and gets out! Then he finds out where I've gone, threatens people who've been good to me, all that. There was once I heard . . . well, it was night, and I heard these noises,

and he was coming through the door with an axe. If I'd stayed there
what was he going to do? After doing that to the front door, what
was he going to do when he came up and found me lying there? Was
he just going to talk to me? Can you see him? So I goes out through
my bedroom window, dropped down on to the low roof of the
kitchen, like, but instead of jumping down from there, I rolled off.
It was about ten or twelve feet to drop. You should have seen me –
and he hadn't touched me!

'I dunno why he does it – my social worker says he's obsessed with
me, or something. It's not doing him any good, this prison, you
know – it's not helping at all. And he's never away long enough
to. . . .

'Sometimes I've wished that when he comes I could stand, you
know? Stand for him to actually get me. But I'm afraid he'll kill me.
And it don't make no difference then – I'm gone. But if I stood
when he comes with the bloody hatchet, and he just gave me another
hammering, then they'd have him. I hope, like, that they'd keep
him for life. . . . But I don't know what he's going to bloody *do* this
time. It's September now, into September, and he's due out on
December 6th. It's gonna come so quick now, you know. It seemed
a long way off when he went in, but it'll soon come. Well, Christmas will soon be here, won't it? Once you get into autumn and
winter, it soon comes round. It's an awful way to live, 'cos you can't
plan nothing. I don't plan nothing. I live from day to day. If he just
vanished off the face of the earth I could be . . . I could be a bit
different from what I am now.'

Keith and Peter rarely played together, even though they could
seem curiously close. Both of them would be gentle with Debbie and
Darren, escorting them to the shop to buy sweets, or simply helping
them play. As soon as Keith came home from school he would be off
– calling for his friends, playing football on the field, or simply
wandering the quiet streets of small, post-war council houses. Peter
would stay around more – less liable to protest when Marion, for the
third or fourth time in the space of two hours, sent him on an errand
for something she had forgotten: a tin of peas, a packet of rice, some
bread.

Marion would shout at him if he had forgotten to take off his
uniform – simply because that uniform, or the part of it he had,
represented much agonizing for her. They were sent a list of seventeen items of uniform (including games clothes) prefaced by the
note: 'All pupils should be dressed in this uniform through their
school career.' Marion's social worker had obtained for her a £16

grant from social security to buy the uniform, but when they went to the shop, they discovered that the blazer alone (first item on the list) was £18. So the trousers, pullover, shirt and tie were all she could buy – and she dreaded Peter's ashamed protests. However, he shrugged and said he didn't mind having less than the other boys. 'But what about next year, when Keith goes?' worried Marion, knowing that the younger boy cared far more for appearances.

Peter was non committal about his fights with Keith. 'Sometimes he starts it, sometimes I do,' he said. 'Mum tells us off, but she don't do nothing really. We have arguments, and we fight. . . . I'm a better footballer than he is. No, he's a better goalkeeper than me, and I'm a better player out than him. I'm good at running, I'm good at cricket, football, rugby, swimming. And I'm good at maths, but I'm better at English. Can't speak English though. I speak Welsh. Don't mean real Welsh. I speak Welsh because I come from Caer-philly.'

Peter talked far more readily – in his sing-song accent – than Keith about the past. 'I remember my first father. I remember when he was having chips and eggs for his tea, and I was naughty, and my father said, No, don't hit him. He was nice; kind. He only ever hit my mother once – in the caravans. He was in work, and my mother was in bed all morning, and she said, You wait till I get up, and he hit her in the mouth and she had to get these two false teeth. . . . I think about him sometimes. Well, it's my mum, you see. She always talks about him, and I thinks about it and cries. Dead people don't go to heaven, do they? My auntie Gloria is dead as well – she died two years ago and my father's been dead seven years now. He crashed coming home, you know. So the man driving was drunk, right? He was drinking and he only had a broken leg, and my father went through the windscreen. Afterwards my uncle Kelvin and Terry and my father's other friends went looking for that man to give him a beating, but he went to live somewhere else and they couldn't find him. . . .

'My second father was all right – I don't know, really – but I don't like him when he hits my mother. He's all right when he hasn't been drinking. It's frightening, horrible, when he smashes things, and that. When we were in bed that night, he came with the hatchet. Did mum tell you? He comes about three o'clock in the morning, and mum fell off the roof getting out of the window, and there was blood everywhere, there was; and in the bedroom he comes and asks Darren, Where is your mother? and Darren says, In there; Debbie got up like a big fool when he come in, to say hallo to him, like.

And when he went in there she was gone out the window, but we could hear her crying because she's hurt herself, and I dunno what happened then – we went next door till the police came.'

Peter grinned and changed the subject: 'I got a girlfriend round here. She's been my girlfriend since yesterday – not yesterday but the day before. Goes to the same school as me. I want to get married when I'm fifteen. And then I'm going to have a couple of pints, but I'm not going to hit my wife.'

Marion: 'I don't know what Keith and Peter's views are – on Davey. I know they didn't like to see him in drink 'cos they were playing out once and he came home drunk at eight o'clock at night, and he was a bit sharp with them like, said, Get up to the house. And I thought, Oh, here we go now. God, you know, I thought the other kids would be laughing at them saying, Is *that* your father? A lot of the kids called him "Davey-hole-in-the-head". I thought, They're going to be stuck with that. I used to worry that they'd have to live up to him – think that because he was a hard nut they'd have to live up to it. I don't think it's a nice thing to be brought up with. I've worried about Keith and Peter a lot. You know, they've been a bit hostile lately – and I couldn't live like *his* mother lived, dreading for one of them to come home. Oh, I couldn't live like that. I'd rather be in a bloody box than live.

'See – the boys need a man around. They feel it in all ways, don't they? Like living down here – they're not posh people down this end of Penarth, they're working-class people. But most of the kids have got fathers that's working, and they can have more or less what they want, ain't it? You know, what kids usually have. They comes in asking for simple things – like Keith likes fishing, and his rod's snapped. He was going sea fishing off the pier and the one he had – it wasn't much – wasn't strong enough. And they were both playing on my nerves asking for these fishing rods, and I said they could have them for their birthdays, in November. You know what I mean – they can't have one just like that, out of one week's money. I just couldn't. . . . So anyway it will have to be second-hand ones. And they won't like that. Because of the other kids, like, and what they have.

'I was looking at my book today – it's going up. I've been on it for two years, so I've just had a rise, a three-pound rise. Now I cash £28.80 a week social security, and £9.20 family allowance. Which, when you think of it, is not a lot of money. Not like what it used to be. I always borrow. Now and again I have a little over, but then I have to get something like a pair of shoes for Darren, and I get a cheap pair — the last ones was £3.49. Then when I do that, and I borrow from next week's for it, I know I'll be in a bloody hole on Monday. I had to fork out £9 yesterday for the television licence, so that was my family allowance gone. When it came to getting Peter's uniform I wasn't going to send him to school, because he didn't have it all. I was just hoping ... I didn't know what was going to happen. Like a windfall might have come out of the sky.

'I'm not normally like this. I like a laugh and all that. But I don't see any future. You know, like thinking of meeting somebody. I think, it can't happen. It's not possible when you've got four bloody kids and you haven't got nothing. It *can* happen; I know it has happened; but I don't think it will ever happen to me. I always dreamt of winning the pools, having a nice house and clothes, and that. No worries. I know when you haven't got money worries you'd have other worries. But I think to myself, if you had enough money – just enough, it would make it a lot easier to worry about anything else then, wouldn't it?

'I do get lonely. It's getting dark nights now, and I'm in here, and I know *he*'ll be out soon, and I'm thinking of what he'll do once he's released. As I say, the kids deserve a bit better. While he's out their life is hell – because I'm waiting, and if I hear a noise at night – oh my God! It's not even very happy when he's inside – all things summed up. You know, they can't have much, and I'm like I am. I've often said they'd be better off in bloody care. They'd get enough good clothes on their back. They wouldn't have me, but then sometimes I wonder if they wouldn't be better off without me. . . .

'I do love them, but I don't show it. No, I don't show it. I don't know why. Well, I used to show it when Peter and Keith were little. When I see other mothers with their children, I know I don't do what they do, like. Debbie *will* come to sit on my lap, but Darren has never been one for being cooched up. Peter and Keith used to like that, and I do remember doing it with them when they were little.

'Oh, I don't know. A lot of it is me. Nobody would take my kids off me. It's not ... well, I ... it's, well, it's because I *do* love them. They know that. Keith hasn't always said it, but in the last few weeks he's said I don't want him and I don't like him. He says it in one of his tantrums. And it's no good me trying to say to him that I *do* want him. I said to him once, if you weren't naughty I'd be different – I wouldn't shout at you or hit you. But whatever I do, he takes it that I don't want him. So now I don't bother explaining to him.'

Keith wanders by the docks in his thin windcheater, brooding about the broken fishing rod he had put back into the cupboard. He is silent most of the time. After a few days the novelty of Peter's new school has worn off, and Keith feels glad that he is still at Cogan Primary. They have scraps up at the big school, he says; soon Peter will be sorry he's gone there. And no, he is not looking forward to moving up himself. At his school he is good at maths, and enjoys the 'SRA' reading scheme, with its coloured cards. But it is hard work at the comprehensive, and 'they have terrorists there'.

Fishing: casting the line, watching and waiting for the bite – only when Keith is thinking about that would his face relax. 'I like fishing because it's a good hobby. You catch a lot of fish sometimes – trout and carp and things like that. When I'm fishing I think about when I will get a thousand fish a day! I like being on me own when I'm fishing. Sometimes when you're down there with friends you talk to them and you have a bite, and then you strike, and the fish gets away because you waited too long. You mustn't just leave it and start reeling, 'cos it'll get away then. You pull on it first, then start reeling, so it hooks then. Yeah, I feel a bit sorry for the fish, but don't mind eating it.

'My mum caught some trout once after she had just got married to my first father. He liked fishing. My mum kept all his stuff, and we would have had it, but then my stepfather sold all my father's fishing stuff. Just got in a mood and sold them. . . . No, I can't remember seeing him – my father. I was only four, or three when he died. I think about him a lot – and I wish he was alive and I could go fishing with him. My stepfather was horrible – he kept on hitting my mum. I hit people because they hit me, but. . . . Well, if he came back tonight I'd go away. Or phone the police. It's just stupidness. Foolish. But I'm frightened of him when he's drunk. And I'd feel awful if he came. 'Cos then he'd come and smash everything up, and all the boys would go: Oh, good God, just *look* at *their* house! They wouldn't think it at the moment because it's all right, but if it does happen, then they will. And it shows me up. All things show me up. Like not having things. And if you lose a ball in football, they shout, You stupid twit. And you feel awful – even you can't help it.

'When I grow up I'll only have a couple of pints. And I'll be nice . . . I'm going in the army then. When I'm thirteen I'll join the young cadets. You can when you're thirteen. Well, you learn there until you're about sixteen, and then you get money to go to the army. You get a thousand pounds. You serve, say, twelve years. And at the end of the time you collect a lot of money, about a million pounds. 'Cos they need an army, you see, for the war, just in case. 'Cos there might be another war. I wouldn't be afraid of fighting, 'cos you gotta learn, haven't you? Being in it, and all? You bayonet sacks; and sometimes there's these posts, and you've got to aim at them, and if you hit the red thing a flag will come up to show you've shot it. Say you hit a certain amount a day, then you pass your tests. It's very difficult, see. If I was in an army I wouldn't just stand there and wait for them to shoot me. I'd shoot them first. There was this film on not long ago, and there was this kid who just wouldn't shoot the other man, so he shot him. He deserved it, didn't he? I think he's a fool. 'Cos in the army they learn, and when they learn they've *got* to do it, they shouldn't just ignore it ... I know it's cruel, but it's got to happen.'

September passed. As Keith's eleventh birthday approached, his relationship with Marion grew worse. One evening he lost his temper and tried to attack her with the poker. Afraid of what she would do to him, she telephoned friends for help, and her social worker spent hours talking to them both. Marion said she wanted to put Keith in care, but the crisis passed. The family made plans about what they would do when 'he' came out, and Keith stayed at home with the rest, waiting.

8 Moya

'The young seagull was alone on the ledge. His two brothers and his sister had already flown away the day before. He had been afraid to fly with them. Somehow, when he had taken a little run forward to the brink of the ledge and attempted to flap his wings, he had been afraid. The great expanse of the sea stretched down beneath and it was a long way down – miles down. He felt certain that his wings would never support him, so he bent his head and ran away back to the little hole under the edge where he slept at night. . . .'

The boy was reading in a flat, monotonous voice. Class 2G listened – less restive than before, when they were exasperated by their religion teacher's attempts to draw a moral from stories of the Wild West pioneers. Their copies of *Saved in Christ* were open at the extract from a story by Liam O'Flaherty; they heard how the young seagull had finally plunged into the void:

' . . . a monstrous terror seized him and his heart stood still. He could hear nothing. But it only lasted a moment. The next moment he felt wings spread outwards . . . he was not falling now but soaring gradually downwards and outwards. He was no longer afraid. He just felt a bit dizzy. Then he flapped his wings once and soared upwards. He uttered a joyous scream and flapped them again. He soared higher. . . .'

The classroom was on the first floor of the school. From the windows a view of grey-green treetops turning brown stretched towards the hills of County Down. Rathmore is a Roman Catholic Grammar School, set well back from the Lisburn Road at the south-west edge of Belfast. It is quite near the controversial Twinbrook estate, originally designed as a "mixed area", but inhabited now by people with serious housing and social problems, mainly younger Catholic families. A small number of pupils comes from the estate; most come from the middle-class Catholic and 'mixed' areas along the Lisburn Road. The school, situated in leafy grounds up a long winding lane, with its teachers dressed in black gowns and its children well-behaved, seems far from the deprivation and hatred of areas like the Falls Road – where little boys who have grown up through the troubles of Northern Ireland learn to throw stones at British soldiers as they learn to walk.

Yet no child in Belfast is immune. Moya, her best friend Maeve, their friends Katrina and Mary and Briege and Niamh, are all twelve – born towards the end of the sixties when the old war in the province flared once more. They complain about their homework, look forward to youth club, chatter about the latest film, ask their parents for more pocket money, and look forward to Christmas, like any other children. But they are also accustomed to the sight of the soldiers in the street, to being searched before entering a department store in the city centre, to bomb warnings, and to the continuous presence of violence. Rathmore's headmistress, Sister Joan Lynam, asserts that 'normality' in Belfast cannot mean what it does elsewhere. Yet Moya shakes her head gently and says: 'That's rubbish. I was brought up here and I don't think I'm too un-normal!' Still, she and her friends readily display their nonchalant bravado to a stranger: 'Were you not afraid to come here? Were you not afraid of bombs? People usually are.'

Moya is a tall thin child with long black hair, a serene expression, and a perfect blend of gravity and gaiety in her nature. She lives with her parents in one of the quiet tree-lined avenues between the Malone Road and the Lisburn Road, a seven-minute bus ride from the school. South Belfast is 'mixed': most of their neighbours are Protestant, and the Malone Road itself was a predominantly Protestant middle-class area until in the last quarter century Catholic families also moved in. Moya's father Hugh describes where they live as 'on the edge of a social precipice', for south of the Lisburn Road the population is mainly working-class and Protestant.

Moya's own home is a rambling detached Victorian house which she shares with her father, a schools inspector, her mother Betty, and her older sister Clare, who is training to be a teacher. Betty is returning to education rather than the Civil Service by taking the Nursery Nurses' Examination Board course. Her six older children have grown up, gone to university and moved away from Belfast. Only Moya's brother Gerry, just married and in his mid-twenties, has stayed in the city – teaching in a Catholic school near the Falls Road.

Hugh and Betty are proud of their eight children. Moya says, 'I'm not boasting but all of them, older than me, they're clever.' Her sisters, Anita, Angela, Marion and Clare, all attended Rathmore before her, so Moya is conscious that she has a tradition to live up to: 'Maeve usually beats me in class – so I come about second or third.

I've got used to it 'cos I don't shine out at any one subject. I'm not shy, you know. But not over-confident. Just kind of in the middle.'

She is one of 876 pupils: 340 boys and 536 girls. Rathmore used to be called the Sacred Heart of Mary Convent Grammar School until eight years ago when boys were about to be admitted, and 'anything to do with a convent put them off'. Sister Joan belongs to the community of thirteen nuns whose convent is next to the school. Six of the staff are nuns; the rest are, with three exceptions, Catholic. This is not policy; as a rule Protestants do not apply for posts. The school has a good academic record and fairly strict rules: the most recent one forbids any child to walk down the long lane to the school alone. There had been too many incidents of boys lying in wait to shout 'Fenian Bastard', and other varieties of abuse, and fight with the Rathmore boys.

Morning: the pupils in their blue uniforms hurry up the lane to the cluster of buildings that make up the school. Moya puffs as usual – she and her friends always complain about the length of the uphill walk from the bus stop. Once a week Father Kelly, parish priest for the area and chairman of the school governors, takes assembly, and the children, with their mixture of awe and affection for him, avoid being late. He stands on the platform in front of the packed hall, as latecomers shuffle in at the back carrying their heavy satchels, briefcases and rucksacks. A sudden silence: 'Hail – Mary – full – of – grace – the – Lord – is – with – thee – Blessed – art – thou – among – women – and – Blessed – is – the – fruit – of – thy – womb – Jesus – Holy – Mary – Mother – of – God – pray – for – us – sinners – now – and – at – the – hour – of – our – death.'

Their heads are bowed. Even the boys at the back cross themselves with respectful precision.

Father Kelly gives his address: 'This week, on October 11th, an announcement was made from the steps of the Vatican to tell the world that we have a new Pope, the 264th successor to St Peter. He is fifty-eight years of age, Cardinal Karol Wojtyla, head of 700 million Catholics, our spiritual head. . . . He is a man with whom the boys especially will identify, as he spends 300 hours a year in sporting activity. He believes that athletic activity should be carried out industriously, and he is a keen skier and mountain climber. Because of this, he communicates easily with youth. His inauguration next week is in the morning so that it may not interfere with those who want to play sport. . . .'

There is no whispering. Those at the back have to strain to hear Father Kelly's voice, but seem interested enough to do so. Then the morning hymn, projected on to a screen on the stage so that they could all read the words, has the melody of a folk-rock song:

> Colours of day dawn in the mind
> The Sun has come up, the night is behind.
> Go down in the city, into the street,
> And let's give the message to people we meet.'

Moya and her class, lined up near the front of the hall, sing enthusiastically, opening their mouths wide, and swaying imperceptibly to the tune.

For their religion period that morning class 2G had been asked by Mr O'Sullivan to prepare little plays about anything they liked. Three boys choose to portray a confrontation between one unbeliever who said 'God is stupid', and two who took exception to this lack of faith. Four girls act out a scene in which beloved Fonzie of the television series died, and found heaven 'cool'. When it came to Moya's table, she, Mary, Katrina and Briege hurry to the front of the class, where Moya poses, hand clasping an imaginary microphone, as a television reporter:

'Good evening, this is Moya reporting from outside Belfast's busy station, where we talk to passengers on the Belfast – Dublin Express where the bombs went off. Now, madam, can you tell me what it was like?' turning to Maeve.

Maeve (in a perfect Manhattan accent): 'Well, I'm just a tourist and I was travelling in the first-class compartment, of course, when I heard this big bang. Then everyone started screaming and you couldn't see anything for the smoke, and it was terrible, really terrible. I mean, I've heard about these bombs, but to really *be* there. . . .'

Moya: 'Thank you, thank you, now what about you, madam. . . .?'

Mary and Katrina each tell the same story. Briege is a woman who had been watching from a window overlooking the railway track. She tells her story in a comically exaggerated Belfast brogue which makes the class smile.

Finally Moya turns to the class, holding the 'microphone' to her mouth: 'Well, we have one dead and many injured, and so far no one has claimed responsibility for this outrage, though police say that two people could have committed it. But who could have put the relatives and friends of these people through all that suffering? This is Moya from Belfast, returning you to the studio.'

The girls look self-conscious and dash back to their seats. To their horror, Mr O'Sullivan insists on discussing their performance: 'Now what do you think was the attitude of those women to the bomb?' The girls bend their heads, looking at each other with expressions of embarrassed irritation. Was it not obvious?

Finally Maeve answers, 'Shock, sir.'

'But do you think any of them might have been glad to be there?' Moya looks down. They fiddle with their pencil cases. Then she shifts her head, with a slightly puzzled, awakening look and says: 'I suppose . . . they could boast about it to people?'

'*Exactly*,' said Mr O'Sullivan, causing Moya to redden. 'Do you not think that some people feel like that when they have been close to disaster, though not affected by it?'

As the group of girls walk down the lane, glad that the day is over, they joke about Mr O'Sullivan: 'H's funny . . . he's so serious. Like when he was asking everybody about their plays. I mean, it wasn't real! He's too serious. He can't seem to take a joke.' Then the conversation turns to violence once more. Moya reminds her friends how one of her brothers had been a front-seat passenger in a car which was fired on, killing the driver's son who was sitting in the back with his friends. Someone else has another tale to tell. Then Moya says, 'And Mary, a man came to your door. He had a gun, didn't he, Mary?' All eyes turn to the quiet girl with short brown hair, who nods.

Suddenly she bursts into tears: 'I . . . don't want to talk about it.' A few minutes later she whispers, 'He was looking for my dad, you see. We'd had these letters which said they were going to burn us out if we didn't move, 'cos it's a Protestant area. It was a year or two ago, but. . . . Anyway, they never found him. But we were so frightened.'

Moya sat at home, in front of the crackling fire in their dining room. She said she had been surprised when Mary started to cry, 'because she's talked about it before. She told us. But maybe she wasn't expecting it . . . I felt sorry for her. I was nearly crying myself. I hate it when people cry. It's horrible.'

She talked quietly about the effects of violence: 'Life has to go on, you know. Once mummy and I were in church, St Bride's, on a Sunday evening. It was dark – must have been winter. We heard a crack like a little toy gun. Then daddy pushed me down under the seat and I was petrified. I said, Daddy, daddy, let's get out of here. The men were at the door of the church, and the man there, he was a part of the church but I can't remember what you call him, threw the collection box at them, and he was shot across the nose. A whole lot of women fainted. The priest who was saying mass went a terrible colour. Outside people were crying, and as daddy took us out we heard a woman crying, My son, my son. Some wicked boys had killed her son and another boy. We came home and had tea, but we felt terrible. But you get over it – it would make your whole life a misery otherwise. So many things happen here, your mind grows numb to it. It dims in your memory.

'You go to town and get used to the soldiers there. I don't know whether they should be here or not, I don't understand it all. You can't be afraid of bombs because usually there are warnings. And you couldn't go to town and stand outside a shop and not go in because you are afraid. You have to go in. Once my friend next door, Nicola, who's Protestant, and I went to town and there was a bomb scare and we got separated in the crowd. But the army defused it. . . .

'Things – the troubles – have got a bit better recently. Apart from the Dublin train it's quietened down a bit in the last two years. Like I told you, I have many friends who are Protestant. I do believe in religion and if anybody said, God's stupid, I would immediately stick up for Him and say, He's not. But I mean sometimes you just kind of . . . like . . . wonder *is* it true? When you hear of people being shot. . . . That *He* would not allow such things to happen – if . . . But I would *try* to understand.

'I think people are wicked when they are just being Protestants out to get Catholics or Catholics out to get Protestants. But when – kind of – it's different. . . . Well, I'm not saying I would *forgive*, but I don't *blame* people so much who have had troubles happen to *them*. Like – their father and uncle and brother have all been shot. It's kind of retaliation. I mean, I don't forgive them and I wish they wouldn't do it, but I just think about it. It's like trials and prisons. I can understand how people act – in a way. I mean, I don't know how I would feel if my brother had been lifted and put in prison, and my father shot, or if all my family had always been pushed around. If it had always been awful for us. . . . You know, *I* might have turned into a terrorist, or something.'

Moya and her friends display no interest in politics. Do they consider themselves Irish? Or British?

Moya shrugged, frowned, and said: 'I don't know; Irish, I suppose. No, both!' She said she loved visiting the Republic of Ireland 'because it's so peaceful there, with none of the troubles,' but added simply that she loved Belfast: Belfast is home. Neither she nor her friends can remember anything other than the shattered city they have grown up in; it is 'normal' to them. But as her parents and teachers point out, what means 'normality' for their generation – the situation before the troubles broke out again in the sixties – was life carried on in an atmosphere of suppressed sectarian tension unknown to any English child. Moya's generation grew up in a frightened city where school tried to preserve the shattered 'normality' by grooming for exams and focusing carefully upon the future. They learnt history in the present of intimidation; mathematics in a world where there was no balance; music to the accompaniment of the tears of children who had seen fathers shot or mothers blown up; religion in towns where the name of God was written in bigoted blood on the walls of slums.

When Moya's older sisters were at Rathmore and she herself was at primary school, none of the educational 'extras' which are taken for granted by English children could take place. No coach trips, no visits to theatres or museums, no after-school extracurricular activities, few sports fixtures with other schools, no youth clubs. Teachers at Rathmore say that the children were, and still are, very different from the past, outgoing generation, who had not suffered from the necessary over-protection: 'They became very weary and did not mature in the same way that children used to. They seemed to have no life in them – it was just as if they were biding their time to get away from all this.'

There are still the bombs, still no resolution. But Moya's tentative suggestion that things might be improving is an instinct shared, though perhaps unexpressed, by her parents and teachers. It is too soon. . . . Yet she can go to the youth club now; her sister Clare can go to visit her boyfriend in the evening, and children from Rathmore *can* stay behind to take part in the activities that go on in any British school. School tests are more dreaded than anything else – as anywhere perhaps, but with an added sense of urgency in Belfast. As one of Moya's teachers remarked: 'Just as they have begun to look forward to a better future the economic depression has set in, making the job and college situation worse.'

When Moya leaves school she may find it even harder to get a place in college than did Clare – already she says she dreads her O-levels and shakes her head wearily at the thought of all the work, using her favourite phrase, 'It's beyond a joke.'

An English lesson: low sun in the room, a crucifix on the wall, and 'I love Maria' carved on a desk. Moya's class was reading *The Taming of the Shrew*. Mrs McClelland reminded them that they had reached the point of Petruchio's marriage, and told them who should read which part. When it came to one passage, one or two of the boys started to nudge:

> This done, he took the bride about the neck,
> And kissed her lips with such a clamorous smack
> That at the parting all the church did echo.

The teacher smiled, directing her remarks to Sean in the front row – the class clown, and a clear favourite: 'Well, I could hope that when you're all married you give your wives a hearty kiss.' As the girls blushed, the boys laughed aloud, making ribald remarks about women.

'I won't have any chauvinism in this classroom,' interrupted Mrs McClelland, causing fresh gales of laughter when she asked, 'What comes after the wedding?'

Afterwards she remarked, 'It's a good book for them to do because it's so amusing. Mind you, some of the remarks in it are a bit embarrassing. And some of the wee girls are very innocent and don't know what it means. The boys do! Some of them giggle, and you can't stop them – though sometimes even I find it embarrassing. . . .'

Moya said, quite seriously, 'Having boys in class is useful sometimes, which is why I wouldn't want to go to a girls' school. They have more courage. Our French teacher said that at our age girls are two years more advanced than boys. But I don't think that's true. There are a good lot of clever boys in our class – and it's to the benefit of the class, you know.'

But there were no boys in choir practice that night. Moya and Maeve and Mary sat with the sopranos on one side of the room, whilst Sister André coached them in a song for Christmas. The room was crowded; girls of all ages sitting on narrow benches, on the floor, on window sills, mouths in perfect O-shapes, eyes fixed upon their teacher. They sang:

> 'The Angel Gabriel came down to visit Galilee,
> And in the town of Nazareth to Mary thus spake he,
> "Among the race of womenkind God's favour thou
>   must bear,
> To thee shall be born a son, a baby king so fair." '

Moya's face, pale and oval, framed by her black hair, was grave.

But Sister André was not satisfied. 'Let's get in the mood, girls. *Think* of our Lady – a simple humble girl. *Think* of the Angel Gabriel. There's no soul in it. You're not *living* it. Live it in your own mind. I can't see the look of awe on your faces at the thought of the Angel Gabriel. It wasn't the postman – it was the Angel Gabriel. You must love it, girls. *Love it!*' That time their voices were sweet, each note held exactly with no slurring – Moya and Mary and Maeve each trying to think of their collective namesake.

On Friday evening there was a different preoccupation. The last lesson of the day had been Irish history, and they had been learning about Irish place names. The lesson had been interrupted by a fifth-form girl who had announced in a monotonous voice: 'There's been an unexploded bomb found in Murray Street, Dunmurry – so anyone who goes home that way should go a different route.' She turned and left the room.

The subdued murmur continued as the children copied out the Irish version of their own names. 'Medh O'Murchadha', wrote Moya's best friend Maeve; Moya was making a cat's cradle in the easy Friday afternoon atmosphere; Mary was wondering what to wear for youth club; not one child thought the bomb warning subject for speculation. It was Friday night, and only that fact interested the class. 'Are you going tonight?' they whispered. 'What are you wearing?' 'Are you going to town tomorrow? What are you going to buy?'

All the way down the lane, all the way home on the bus, Moya and her group discussed the merits of culottes or dresses or straight cord jeans. When Moya arrived home she continued the speculation over her evening meal – whilst her father, mother and older sister listened to her. 'But *what* shall I wear, Clare?'

Clare, nineteen years old with black hair flowing down her back, shrugged and smiled, 'I really don't know, Moya.'

'Can I look in your wardrobe?'

'Well, you can look, and if you find something you like I *might* let you wear it.'

'Oh, Moya,' said her mother, who was dressed elegantly herself, 'you've got lots of pretty dresses.'

'But they don't dress up at the youth club. Not for the disco dancing. I'm going to wear my straight blue cord jeans, and one of Clare's tops.'

When Maeve arrived Moya was dressed in Clare's pale blue sweatshirt, and her pale blue laced suede shoes, with her own jeans – and she was worried about the combination. But Maeve, was admiring:

'Oh you look really nice, Moya – *really* nice.'

There was a rattling sound in the air around the house; a monotonous threatening whirring. Hugh pointed from the back door:
'Look, that is one of the sights and sounds of Belfast,' as the search-
light beam from the hovering helicopter moved from right to left,
piercing the darkness.

The two girls walked up the road to their youth club with the
thing still hanging overhead, and Moya shivered: 'I suppose we
should be used to it, but I don't like it. It's creepy – horrible.' As
the girls crunched past the Ulster Defence Regiment post, kicking
up the leaves and peering up at the watchtower to see if they could
see a soldier, they heard the faint sound of an accordion from inside
the high fence. It sounded thin and melancholy. 'Perhaps they're
having a party,' said Moya.

The craze was disco dancing. Each Friday night a score of boys put
on their jeans and T-shirts, and went to the youth club to pretend to
be John Travolta. The girls were amused by their new attempts at
dancing: 'They would never have had the courage were it not for
"Saturday Night Fever".'

Maeve and Mary and Moya lined up with the other children as a
man in tight beige trousers, with hair in a semi-fifties cut, taught
them the intricacies of disco routines. 'Right, are you ready? Forward two three four, step, click, punch and *turn* – side-two-three,
back-two-three, walk two-three-four – *turn* – Now you should all be
facing this way. . . .'

Moya and Maeve looked helplessly at each other. Moya had ended
up in the right position; Maeve had not, Mary caught up just in
time. They giggled. 'Now, shall we try it to music?' The sound of
the Bee Gees filled the room; the pace was faster; the children's legs
got mixed up as they scurried in obedience to the shouted instructions. The girls laughed at each other.

Later, growing tired, they sat in the coffee bar room upstairs
eating crisps and complaining about their homework – 'We have so
much to do there isn't time to *think*' – before rushing down to join
the dancers once more. Moya's parents collected them. A year or so
ago they would not have been allowed to youth club at all.

It was cold on Saturday; Moya stayed in bed till late morning,
unwilling to rise even then. There was a fire in the dining room,
mist on the windows, grey damp air outside. After lunch Maeve
called for her once again, and they walked to the nearby sports hall
for their regular Saturday afternoon badminton session. Voices
echoed in the cold room, lit by a cracked skylight. Four or five

games were in progress. The girls put their name tags on the board, so that when the bell went they would get a court, taking pot-luck as to who their partners would be. Then they played for twenty minutes till the bell went again, re-entering their names on the board, so that in the afternoon they could play about four times. Once Moya had to play with three boys and she blushed, walking reluctantly to join them.

The organizer smiled: 'We have terrible problems at this age in trying to get the girls to play with the boys. If two boys draw against two girls they won't split up and play mixed doubles. And the girls hate being with three boys, and vice versa. They get so embarrassed.'

After Moya's game she sat on a bench with her friends, talking about the Jane Fonda film 'Barbarella' which they had all been allowed to stay up and watch after youth club the night before. They were scathing: 'It was ridiculous, childish, just foolish,' said Moya.

'I thought Jane Fonda was supposed to be a good actress,' said Maeve. 'Anyway, when was it *made*? When I was about two!'

Moya asked, 'Why do you think it was given an X?'

Maeve looked coy, in a knowing sort of way, but Moya was dismissive: 'Oh, *that*! Well, we all know about *that*! And those stupid clothes she wore − if that's supposed to be *sexy*. . . . I think they should have put it out at four in the afternoon for the children, not last thing at night.'

It was growing dark by the time the session ended. Moya walked along the road with Mary, Briege and Maeve, swinging her racket, and gossiping once more about school − too much homework, favourite teachers, coming half-term tests. They stopped at a garage to buy sweets, and walked along chewing − faster than the group of older girls in front, who had also been playing badminton. They were laughing noisily. 'Go on, Eileen, you know you fancy him. You do! Go on, Eileen, he lives *that* way − I dare you!' The girl in question, dark-haired and red-cheeked, flounced across the road, followed by cat-calls. Moya's little crowd overtook them, falling silent as they passed. In admiration Moya whispered, 'They're *much* older than us − they're about fifteen.'

Moya said that she sometimes likes the thought of growing up, but sometimes not. 'When I see Clare going out with high heels and makeup and clothes I kind of envy her. But I don't fancy having to go through O-levels and A-levels − I'm dreading it already. I want to do well. I wouldn't say I'm in competition with my family, but I wouldn't like to be the only one who only got one A-level. Anyway, they give us a lot of tests at school. We have them at Christmas and little ones at half term, and really important ones at Easter. You have a special exam room where you're so many metres apart. You have two tests every day, and have your dinner in between. Two tests a day, on the whole year's work! It's beyond a joke. Last year I did my revision the night before. But, you see, the teachers give you homework right up till then. You would think that two weeks before the test they'd give you none! Oh, I don't mind school. Once you get there it's not too bad, but I don't know anybody who thinks, Oh goody, Monday morning, it's lovely getting up at eight o'clock; great to have loads of homework!'

She sat curled up in front of the fire, holding a Snoopy doll, excited at the prospect of seeing one of her older brothers, Paul, who was coming that evening for a visit before leaving for England to train as a pilot for Aer Lingus. 'I used to be the baby of the family, but I'm not so much now. The other's have all gone – there's only me and Clare left. It's funny – I'm an aunt to six children, at my age!

'I can remember my first day at school. It's funny I remember it. It's a funny thing to remember. I was walking with Clare. She was at the same school. She was in P7, huge big P7, and I was going into P1. When I was walking along I got a stone in my shoe, and that's the one thing that has really stuck in my mind. The stone in my shoe. It's funny. And I had to stop; I was trying to put if off for as long as possible, but the stone hurt, so I had to stop and get it out. I had to stand there, and Clare walked on. Maybe I was afraid of being late, but I cried because I was left. It's funny – how can you remember something as daft as a stone in your shoe? When you forget other things that are more important?

'And I remember something before that. I must have been about four – a little Spotty Muldoon I was called, in my spotted bathing suit. I was just a little babe, but it kind of stuck in my memory: I was at this seaside resort and going for a paddle. I looked round and I couldn't see mummy or daddy, because the tide was a long way out, and you had to walk quite a bit, so I'd walked away from them. And I looked round and I looked and I couldn't see them. They were sitting in the rocks somewhere and I couldn't see them. I was frightened when I couldn't see my parents. It was probably the first time I'd been alone – with so many brothers and sisters. I remember crying. I remember the fear because I couldn't see my parents.

'I think Bernard's lucky (you know, he's my eldest brother – he's about thirty I think) because he's got a wife and he's got children, and mummy and daddy are still – you know – alive. They're not young and they're not old – they're just kind of . . . mummy and daddy, you know, that age. But maybe by the time I'm his age, mummy and daddy won't be alive. To help me and see my children. Between Bernard and mummy and daddy there isn't a big age gap, but there is between me and mummy and daddy. So they can go out together when he visits us to have drinks and a good time. But by the time I'm grown up they might not want to. I might only be young when they die. It makes me sad to think of that. But it has crossed my mind.'

9 *Melanie*

You wouldn't pick her out from the 1050 pupils streaming into Dearneside Comprehensive in the morning. A little slimmer perhaps, prettier than most, and with an expression that does not hate the thought of school – or hate the thought of anything. Melanie Cook walks to school quite happily, daydreaming about her coat. The Coat. It will be black leather, close fitting, and fall to within six inches of her ankle. There will be a split up the back from hem to waist. And, most important, the front bodice will be pin-tucked from shoulder to waist. Definitely not plain: they are not wearing them plain. And the belt will be tied behind, perhaps even with a necktie knot, and allowed to hang down over the split. That coat will feel soft to the touch, and smell good, of real leather. Walking to school in her brown school mackintosh, Melanie knows that when she gets The Coat everyone will tell her she looks great. She can even hear them now.

'Me mum's going to get me a leather coat for Christmas,' she whispers to her friend Shiela. 'We went into Doncaster on Saturday and saw them. There were some at £39, but they weren't so nice. She says we can go again. And I know what she'll do. We'll try one on I like, then she'll sneak back and ask them to put it on one side. She's done it before – I've seen her. Oh, but what I really want to go with it are them black boots with spurs on. And for the Christmas party I'm having one of them tweed gathered skirts with a waistcoat to match, and a shirt with a tie. It's all the fashion. They're wearing ies at t'youth.'

Shiela listens, impressed. The subject is endless. Melanie and her friends, like a thousand other thirteen-year-old girls, fill the corners of their day with thoughts of the night, clothing their fantasy selves like the teen models in *Jackie* and *Oh Boy*.

They live in Goldthorpe, in South Yorkshire. It is a large village – or small town – roughly halfway along the straight main road that runs from Barnsley to Doncaster. The small cluster of shops, two banks, police station, two schools, pubs and workingmen's clubs, is surrounded by collieries. The six, called Highgate, Goldthorpe,

Hickleton, Barnburgh, Manvers Main, and Wath Main, provide employment for most of the men of Goldthorpe and the surrounding area. The beautiful bleakness of the landscape around the town is broken by the jagged outlines of pithead gear on each horizon.

Most of the boys will leave Melanie's school and follow their fathers down the pit, just as her own brother Stephen has done. Most of the girls at her school will marry miners, just as her mother did. Nearly all the kids were born in the small area – as Melanie was, in her grandmother's house – and will always live there.

When Melanie links arms with her friend Tina to roam the streets every night, they moan a little about the lack of things to do, but not with much conviction. They accept Goldthorpe. They stare in at the lighted shop windows, looking at the cheap trinkets, china ornaments, plastic handbags in polythene bags, vinyl purses, novelty key rings, and tiny silver-look earrings, and get to know each window display by heart. 'It's all right,' says Melanie, 'but I wish it weren't so dirty. It's right scruffy – look at all the rubbish and dirt in the streets. It's t'pits make it dirty. But apart from that it's all right. We've some nice shops. . . . I don't want to move, or owt like that.'

It was 31 October, Halloween, the night when children in the North of England go out 'mischieving' in the streets. Melanie walked quickly home from school, and turned into Kelly Street where the small red-brick terraced houses are threatened by subsidence. Already houses in the next street are showing jagged cracks caused by the ground shifting over the carved-out coal faces far below. She pushed open the door of their house, which open straight into the best sitting room, and burst into the back living room-kitchen where her father was home and her mother was making sandwiches for tea. 'Hey up!' was her greeting, the same every night, the same tone, as if nothing in the world could depress her.

Eric and Pat Cook are in their early forties. Pat works part-time in a bread shop; Eric has worked down the mine since he left school twenty nine years ago. He started as a faceworker, but the last eleven years he has been a deputy, which means that he is in charge of the safety and welfare of the men working in a particular district of the mine. It is a semi-official job; deputies are not in the National Union of Mineworkers, nor at the level of management, but somewhere in between: a sometimes uneasy but responsible position. He earns a good wage (around £5000 a year) and owns their little house, which is worth about £4000, or less because of the subsidence. Eric and Pat have been on the council list for years, because they want 'a bigger place with a proper kitchen'. But they do not worry about money, or houses. As long as there is enough money to buy seventeen-year-old Stephen a stereo for Christmas, and get Melanie The Coat, and have a holiday next year (the first time abroad) in Majorca, they are content.

'All the kids are out mischieving,' said Melanie, coming downstairs in her jeans. 'They'll be rattling the door in a minute.' She lit candles inside the two jack o' lanterns – hollowed-out turnips with demoniac faces – and her dad switched off the light for a moment so that their eyes and mouths gleamed.

Pat, a quiet pretty woman who wore high stiletto heels even to cook supper, reminded her daughter that she had to babysit that night.

'Yes, but I'm going out mischievin' first,' replied Melanie, disappearing through the back door. Out along the 'backins' (the alley that runs between two rows of houses) in the darkness, hearing the voices of children giggling, the echo of running feet. . . .

'Melanie, Melanie!' It was David, and Tina, and David's cousin, Stephen, detaching themselves from the gloom to greet her.

'I'm not goin' babysittin' while eight o'clock,' said Melanie. So the little gang ran off, ringing doorbells and running away, rattling letter boxes, and uttering odd little yelps and laughs to make any old-age pensioner nervous. Other children passed them, some little girls even dressed as witches. The night was filled with fun, fright, and naughtiness, and the kids loved it. Melanie was sad when she had to walk two streets for her babysitting duty. Yet in that house too the turnip heads were hung in the kitchen, and though the three children were fast asleep, they all woke during the evening, crying because they had been dreaming of wicked witches.

Next morning, as Melanie walks to school with the rest, her headmaster, Mr Dickinson, was already seated at his desk. The administrative problems of running a large school like Dearneside are considerable. Mr Dickinson wears a habitually worried expression as he copes with the complex timetable, a lack of space, inevitable absences amongst staff, and uncompleted building work. Dearneside Comprehensive was built in 1936 as a secondary modern, with separate boys' and girls' departments. They were merged in 1963, and with comprehensive reorganization the numbers increased from 750 to 1050. As a secondary modern the school was run on traditional lines; as a comprehensive it has not changed: 'We still insist on a uniform inside school, to give a feeling of belonging, of dignity. Also it makes it easier for families to get help. We have 150 families receiving grants from the local authority for uniform. We still have corporal punishment in the school; we say that the children must walk on the left of the corridors – that sort of thing.'

There is no sixth form at Dearneside; those who wish to take A-levels go to the sixth-form college at Mexborough. Each year, out of the 200 pupils who leave at sixteen, twenty go there, and a further twenty take courses (typing, catering, etc) at a technical college. Of the other 160, Mr Dickinson says that most of the boys will go down the pit, or to the steelworks; the girls will travel to factories or shops in Doncaster, Rotherham and Sheffield.

'There is not much else for them to do,' Mr Dickinson admits. 'In school we have more children in the low ability range than the high ability range; a higher proportion of children in need of remedial assistance than the national average. The people who want choice as to jobs have to move out of the area – which continues the cycle of deprivation of those who are left.'

The headmaster says that his main problem is not discipline, or truancy, or lack of funds – though they all play a part. 'The worst thing is apathy – a failure to see the value of education. The parents tell them, I'll be glad when you're earning, and ask me, Can my son leave as soon as he's sixteen, without even wanting him to finish his CSEs.'

Melanie is sitting in her maths class, tucked away in the centre of the room with Shiela, Diane and Julie. The teacher is writing something on the board: 'Now, what do you do if you are making shoes? Do you make a lot of a big size, or a lot of a little size? No, what you do is look for the size shoe most people take. And what do you call that?'

'Av-er-age,' they chorus.

'Right, now we're going to learn how to work out the mean – or average. . . .'

From the classroom windows there is a view of misty hills, broken by a smoking chimney. The afternoon is warm, the classroom close. Melanie, like all the other girls, is wearing a midcalf grey pleated skirt, with a pale blue blouse and a royal blue cardigan. Some of them wear ankle socks, most blue or white knee socks, with heavy black flat sandals – the latest fashion. Their clothes make them look fragile, like refugees in charity garments, or dowdy waifs from an Edwardian orphanage. The boys look tougher in their baggy black pants, buttoned at the waist and tight over the bottom, showing scuffed Dr Martins boots. All of them wear ties – a rule about which Mr Dickinson is most strict. They are oddly assorted – some boyish, some lanky with spots, faint moustaches, and breaking voices. Melanie's class looks a strange mixture of children and teenagers, an awkwardness reflected in self-conscious clumsy movements and easy embarrassment.

After maths it is French. Melanie hates French. As usual she bows her head in the midst of a knot of girls, hoping she will not be asked to read. Mrs Thistlewood has written ten sentences on the board for them to translate, with a full vocabulary list beside. When a boy is asked to read, performs well, and is rewarded by two House points, there is a dark mutter of 'show-off' from elsewhere in the room.

Lanky Leslie Wall is unruly, shouting out, 'Hey, miss, can you get done for chopping down a telegraph pole?' When Elaine is asked a question because she has not put up her hand, her neighbours nudge and grin at the singling out – any singling out. She answers perfectly.

The teacher is exasperated: 'You see, you *do* know! You just can't be bothered. You're too shy.' Whilst the class is struggling through the translations in comparative silence, she whispers: 'It is frustrating teaching a class like this. They won't do French after this year so that will be it. They come to me and say, I'll never go to France, miss, so what's the point? Or, My dad says all I'll ever need to know is pit talk. It's terrible. Sometimes I wonder what I'm doing it for – plodding on.'

As they walk from lesson to lesson the girls, always with their best friends, gossip about clothes and boys. The boys, less attached to each other, laugh and push. In the chemistry laboratory they do not alter their behaviour and when their teacher, a tall, quiet-voiced man, informs them that they are to go to the visual aids room for a film about the basic elements the noise increases. He remonstrates. They take no notice. Forced to raise his voice he looks frustrated: 'I *told* you to be quiet. Now I don't want to be bawling and shouting at you. Walk quietly along the corridors. . . .' But they make more noise than ever, banging and rasping their chairs on the floor of the television room, which is directly above the headmaster's study.

Frustrated, the teacher shouts again: 'You've shouted and screamed along the corridor, you've made a noise in here when I've asked you not to. It's impossible to treat you decently because you don't respond.' Silence. A boy blows his gum out into a bubble until it collapses with a gentle 'plop'. One or two of the girls look at each

other from beneath swinging fringes and grin. But Melanie is staring at the teacher with an expression of concern. She feels sorry for
him — she is thinking that the rest of the class are awful to him, but
it is his own fault in a way: he is too soft.

When at last the video recorder is switched on, the class settle
down. Then, accompanied by lively music, the title comes up: 'A
PERIODIC TABLE'. Shaun sniggers, and nudges the girl next to him.
She looks half embarrassed, half amused, and in turn nudges her
friend. There is a ripple through the rows, a gleam of grins. Then
the mutter and shuffle, kick, whisper and scrape, as the bright voice
introduces them to hydrogen and helium. About half the class listen
and watch attentively, though it is hard to tell whether this is
through real interest, or due to the habitually hypnotic effect of the
TV screen. A shot of a baby being breast-fed sets the boys off again,
but draws a whispered 'Aaah' from some of the girls. 'Shurrup,
Shaun,' snaps Elaine at last, irritated by his sniggers.

Music: they have to cross the windy yard to an annexe, where an
upright piano stands in one corner of the small stale room. The boys
sit one side, the girls the other. Mr Spink, a small bearded man with
an addiction to the loud pedal and obvious enthusiasm for his subject, gives out song books called, *Fun with Tunes*. 'The boys will
sing, 'Come, Landlord, Fill the Flowing Bowl', whilst the girls
tackle, 'There is a Tavern in the Town' — at the same time. You'll see
how they go together.'

They look at him in disbelief — rightly as it turns out, for the
noise is appalling. The girls laugh as they lose their places. Only
David, in the front row, an obvious ex-choir boy despite his broken
voice, sings with conviction.

Their teacher protests: 'The idea of doing anything like this is
that you're working in a team. You're helping other people. If you're
digging a hole and just lean on your shovel, you don't deserve to be
paid on Friday. If you're singing in parts and don't do your bit, it's
not going to sound nice. . . .' Finally he gives up, and runs through
the hymn they are learning for assembly. It is 'Jerusalem'. Together,
class 39 sing their question:

> 'And did the Countenance Divine
> Shine forth upon our clouded hills?
> And was Jerusalem builded here
> Among these dark Satanic Mills?'

As the bell rings for the end of the lesson, Mr Spink stands before
them, waving his hands, reassuring them: 'Beautiful words, beauti-

ful tune. "Till we have built Jerusalem" – it's up to you to do that, you know. You're the kind of people who can do that. You can.'

Melanie rarely gets into trouble. She labels the girls who do as 'bad uns', but likes them just the same. Proud to have been voted a monitor, she likes to be liked. As she is. 'I like being in my class – most of them are right nice. We're in the average group: 3, 3.3 and 3.4 are top classes in t'third year, so they haven't got nowt to do with us, like. Everything what they do is different. German, and stuff like that. Us – 3.9 – we're all average. In maths I'm above average – I'm in t'top group for maths, but in all the rest average. I like doing graphs and things like that – sort of sadistics, or whatever you call it. There's more kids average than what there is above average. I think I'd rather be average 'cos I can keep up with what they're doing, and I'm not below. If I were in a higher group I'd be below all the time, because they'd be ahead. When you're average they don't call you "brainy", and things like that – Oh, she's better than t'others.' She mimics a jeer. 'I wouldn't like that. I wouldn't like to be brainy, 'cos they expect more from you when you're brainy. I'm not clever at all.

'In French last year I did bad – below average. Me other subjects – some were good, some bad. I didn't do much revision for the exams last year. I couldn't be bothered. I went out with all t'kids ... so.... But this year I'm going to revise more because third year exams count more. 'Cos at the end of the year we pick what subject we want to take for rest of t'time at school. Counts on your job, y'see. You've got to take maths and English. And I'll take rural studies and community service – helping old people and things like that. And I'm taking cooking and sewing. They're good for jobs, both of them. And if I want to be a nanny, helping old people is similar, isn't it?

'I love kids. I want two of me own, a boy and a girl. When I'm about twenty three. I don't want to get married while [until] I'm twenty. There's a lot get married at eighteen and nineteen here. It's stupid, 'cos they see no life, do they? They just have one boy, and that's it. Stuck in all the time. I like to go out with me mates and have good fun. But there's nowt to do when you leave school. Nearly all goes in t'factories, and the boys go in t'pits.

'Factory must be horrible – stuck all day with all t'machines, doing all t'things over and over again. I'd rather work in a shop in town – at least you meet people. If I can't be a nanny I'll do that.

What I'd really like to be is a model, but I won't try for that. I don't tell my friends – they'd call me big-headed. Do you have to be clever, to be a model? They're right fashionable. Or a dancer. I've always wanted to be a dancer, but I don't think I've got no chance. You have to be able to sing. But I'd love to be. I think it's great. When you're watching t'musicals and things like that, and you see them on stage with all those lovely clothes and all. When I were in pantomime last year I used to dance in front of people. I were one of t'main dancers, and used to love it. For them two weeks . . . getting all t'makeup on, and all t'clothes, and hearing them clapping, . . . But towards the end you got fed up. None of me mates was doing it. I were getting too old for it 'cos you had to do young things. You had to pretend you were a fairy.'

Melanie Cook wants to grow up. 'I wish I was sixteen. I started – you know – my period last week. No, it were two weeks ago. They tell you about periods in your first year. The science teacher. But the lads are there as well. I felt stupid when they were telling us and all t'lads were there. All of us were going red. It's silly them laughing – mum said it were. Them that had started felt embarrassed. But that time I hadn't started. I'd been poorly a few weeks ago and the doctor told me I were ready for it. I was glad when I did, 'cos you see a lot of girls in our class had started, and you feel more grown-up when you have. Now in our class there's only about three that haven't. My cousin, she's fifteen, and she only started two weeks before me, and she were upset about it, you know. 'Cos she was the last of her mates.

'Me mum keeps saying that about clothes – that I want to be older. I like clothes and fashion, and me mum says I want to be sixteen. I *wish* I was. I want to go places . . . you can get married at sixteen, can't you? I won't. There's a girl in the fourth year, or she should be – she's left school a year early, and she's had a baby. She's married. She's only two years older than me. Oh, it's a shame really. You see her, and she doesn't look old enough to have a baby. And her husband – he's nineteen. Stupid. It's daft. They'll be fed up with each other by the time they're thirty. They'll have a long time together, all of them.'

All week Melanie was looking forward to her perm. By the time Thursday came, excitement had toppled over into fear: what would it look like? Her straight brown bob would be crinkled into a frame of curls, just for £4. But what if it looked daft? What if she walked into school and the others laughed at her? What if it turned out wrong? Melanie could hardly eat her bacon sandwich before walking down the dark road, past the Cheap Shop, and along to Miles Hair Fashions next to the Rave Cave, her favourite boutique.

Up the narrow stairs, then bent back over a basin, feeling the ache in her neck, and the shiver of cool water. A towel wrapped round, staring at herself in the mirror, frowning slightly at the embarrassing baldish reflection. A small thin face, her father's almost-hooked nose, light brown eyebrows. . . . Then the smell of permanent wave lotion, the tight pulling so that her head nearly ached, the waiting with the lotion growing colder and colder, before the welcome warmth of the dryer. At last the curlers were unwound, the brush whisked round her head – and there she was. Melanie stared. From a smooth crown a circlet of curls framed her face. But she had wanted the fringe left straight, not permed . . . it wasn't quite right. For a moment she felt worried – but the image before her was reassuring. Melanie smiled. The perm looked good.

Eric did not like it. 'I'm old-fashioned – me. I like girls with the long straight hair, like they used to wear it.'

But Pat was relieved, 'It looks nice, Melanie, better than how it was.' Every five minutes she would gaze self-consciously in the mirror over the mantelpiece, fiddling with the tendrils of hair that now sat with an odd lightness around her head. The next hurdle was the third-year Halloween party, to be held in the school hall that evening. In the afternoon her class had scrubbed and prepared the potatoes for baking – 'rosties', they called them. Melanie was nervous now – what would the others think?

'Melanie will wear anything as long as it's the latest fashion,' Eric Cook said once, but it was not true. She worried desperately about what the other girls would think, what they would wear, whether she would be the same as them. 'When one gets something, they all want one. You don't want to be different. Like the coat. Everybody's getting them so I want one. The same style. I'm not bothered what I look like, as long as it isn't *old fashioned*.'

So to go to the school dance she wore her straight cord jeans – no dreadful mistake like wearing flares was possible. And as she entered the dark school hall, lit with the jack o' lanterns and decorated with pictures of witches, the little gasps from her friends made her grow pink and grin: 'Oh, Melanie, your hair. It looks right nice, it does, Melanie.'

The girls danced round in the dark, gathered in huddles to whisper – and stared at boys they liked. When slow music came on they even did 'the creep' together. The boys clowned – only one or two daring to dance, or even to sprawl uncomfortably with girls on their knees. But when the games teacher asked for relay teams to snatch apples from bowls of water, even the most sophisticated girls raced to the front, long hair tumbling into the water, faces pink. The lights went down again, the deafening music glazed their minds, until it was time for the buttery potatoes, and hunks of 'parkin' (ginger cake). Then they became children again, not minding if the food smeared on their clothes. One or two teachers who had come surveyed them fondly. 'Oh, it's a lovely daft age, the third year,' said one.

Friday morning. 'Oh, Melanie, what've you done to your hair?' jeers Leslie Wall (whom Melanie used secretly to like) showing by his smile that he approved. But Melanie stares enviously at Mrs Braithwaite, their form teacher – a tall, striking young woman with a very pretty face, and a mass of reddish hair in a curly frizz.

'It i'nt right. I wish it were like Mrs Braithwaite's,' she mutters, pulling perpetually at her fringe, ruffling up the sides, so that in silhouette she resembled a thirties-style doll. 'I don't like it. I wish it were different' . . . and she frowns, the expression unusual upon her face.

Their music teacher seems cross, too, his humour not helped by the distinctly cold wind that cuts through the crevices of his little annexe room, which seems as if it had been temporary several years ago. He passes back a pile of homework books, angry that the work has not been completed properly. The boys and girls open the pages at the fuzzily drawn crochets and quavers in the wrong places on their ruled-out lines. Mr Spink is shouting at them: 'You just don't bother. It's becoming increasingly difficult to treat anybody decent, because you know if you do they won't bother. Born messers-about – all of you. You're going to end up on the street corner waiting for the social security place to open. It's a good enough place for those that need it, but it's not a good place if you go there through idleness. You want to grow up decent useful citizens whose brains work, no matter what the subject is. . . .'

They stare at him. Then Shaun, one of the more difficult boys in the class, puts up his hand. 'It's because it's homework, and – be honest, sir! – we don't like homework. We want to go home and watch telly.'

Mr Spink's voice takes on a note of desperate persuasion: 'That's where you're wrong. You're learning from the day you're born till the day you die. And homework is very beneficial. . . .'

'It all goes in one ear and out the other,' says Melanie. 'It doesn't worry anybody when he tells us all off like that. Nobody minds. What's worse is if he picks on one person who's done it well, and he might give them House points. The rest of 'em don't like it then. They might take it out on him. Kids are cruel – kids our age. They take it out on people. Like there's kids at our school who come in right funny clothes, old pumps, and things like that. And you feel right sorry for them. There's a girl in our class, and she's a bit cross-eyed. She had to go to hospital for her eye, and I feel right sorry for her. She hasn't got much. Her clothes aren't very with it, and things like that. When she comes to school in trousers they're all creased up and too short for her. The boys in our class tease her and she starts crying. They call her 'The Scruff' – 'cos she's not well dressed. She's all right, but she does look right dopey, with glasses on t'end of her nose. And they say she smells, and things like that. Oh, I feel *right* sorry for her.

'There's a lot of people in school like that. Right funny. Some people look like they've got their mum's coat on. There was this one girl, and she had one of them coats with fur round in red, what old grandmas wear, and oh, everyone was looking at her and laughing at her – and I felt awful for her. When I see. . . . Well, I feel sorry for a lot of people. Me mum's sentimental like that. When I see people who's poorly, like on films, I cry. In 'Roots', when I see them being whipped, I cry. And sometimes horrible films of people starving – the little children. It shows how lucky we are. Shows how much we have, doesn't it? I wouldn't stop crying if I saw anything like that. I wouldn't stop thinking of it. But I don't see why they have to live in those countries. Why can't they come over here? Why can't we send them food? 'Cos, I mean, we throw things on back of t'fire what could save somebody's life, couldn't it? Oh, it's funny.

'But then I suppose people wouldn't want them here. Some people say black is rubbish and we don't want them in our country. There's a boy in our year – not in my class – and they all call him "nigger". He's dark, but he's not black, he's brown. You know, he's not as dark as . . . they can be. They call him things like that – Sambo. I think it's cruel. So we call them Sambos or chocolate drops, and they call us white drops? It's stupid just the same. They're the same as us but just different coloured skin. I don't know why people hate them. Same as when Goldthorpe and Thurnscoe fight. You know, it's t'next town, and the gangs fight. 'Cos they're living in a different place! It's daft. They should all go round together. But if Thurnscoe lads see a lad from Goldthorpe, they'll give him a beating. Yeah – kids are cruel: the things they do and say to people. And it's only at people who are different. Like some, when they've got to have free school dinners, and you have a line through the dinner ticket so they'll know in the kitchen. And the others tease them and say they can't afford to have dinner, you see. Horrible. But it's natural. I tease people sometimes! And we all talk about each other behind backs – say, She's horrible, and things like that.

'It's nice when you're popular with people. When they all say, Melanie, come with us, and, Let Melanie sit there, and things like that. It's nice when they all want you and they're not leaving you out: Oh, we don't want her coming. Once, when I was in the juniors I moved up into a different class, and I didn't know many people, and they all sat me on this table and they were all picking on me, and I didn't like it. They were all my friends later, when they got to know me. But when you think you're sat all on your own, it's horrible. And some people are always like that, aren't they?'

It took some confidence to go to Goldthorpe Youth Club, and none of the lonely girls and boys, the teased ones, the bullied ones, the poorer ones from Melanie's class ever went. 'They wouldn't have owt to wear,' said Melanie, with an expression of resigned sadness. For her the big decision, of course, was which clothes to choose, and through the lessons on Friday (apart from the fascinating physics experiments which gripped the whole class) she worked it out, with the precision of a General masterminding his campaign.

As soon as she got home she asked, 'Dad, have you got any old neckties?' Eric went upstairs to see and came down with a handful of narrow, silky things in bilious colours which set her off into spasms of giggles: 'Did you *wear* these?'

Pat was cooking tea; the tiny room was warm as darkness fell outside. Melanie sifted through the ties, finally choosing an old plum and white-striped one. 'If I wear me tweed skirt it's got some red in it, and I'll wear me simon shirt, and t'tie, and me new white socks and me soul sandals.' Friday night was disco night at t'youth, so appearance was crucial.

The fire was roaring, the back boiler shut down for Melanie's bath. As she was upstairs preparing herself, her brother Stephen came in – a tall, gauche boy of seventeen, with his own hair newly permed. Stephen works as an apprentice fitter in the same pit as his father, and was studying his pay slip. There was something on it he could not understand, although the total after deduction – £38.50 – seemed correct.

Eric shook his head: 'I've explained it all to you, Stephen. Time you worked it out yourself. You don't live to work – you work to live, don't forget it. You go down t'pit for money, and you just learn to see how much they've given you. 'Cos if they've made a mistake *they* won't tell *you*. You get back to that window next day and tell them till they've got it right, lad.' The buff envelope went into the best china cabinet with his own. 'Hey up!' She came into the room and twirled round.

'You look nice, Melanie,' said Eric, looking fondly at his daughter, who resembled a fifties teenager in her socks and full skirt.

Stephen guffawed, 'No, she don't, she looks right stupid!'

'Take no notice of him, love, you look right nice.' Melanie met a new friend from Thurnscoe before walking to the youth club. She had met Debbie two weeks earlier, at half term, when they were both earning some extra money by picking potatoes. She explained that Debbie's mother lived alone with her three children – 'She's got no dad, like, so she was working for money to give her mum to help with the Christmas presents.'

Debbie was one year older than Melanie, tall and extremely pretty, with waist-length straight hair. She shivered at the thought of entering the youth club: butterflies . . . wondering who would be there. And as they approached the building, where knots of youths and girls hung around, waiting for it to open, both girls began to shiver – trembling and hunching their shoulders. 'Ooh, it's cold.' But it was nothing to do with the wind, though both wore short-sleeved T-shirts under their thick jackets.

'I'm scared, Melanie, I'm terrified to go in,' said Debbie.

'So am I,' groaned Melanie. 'I feel daft with me hair. I think I'll take this tie off. Do'y think they'll be wearing ties?' They approached two older girls who huddled smoking in a doorway. They both wore identical black leather coats with pin tucks and back splits from waist to hem, and they each dragged fiercely on an Embassy, held between finger and thumb.

Melanie was pleased to talk to them; it made her feel older, accepted. Then she whispered, 'Some of me friends smoke, and they all go on to me, Have a drag, go on, have a drag, then they say, Oh, little angel, and you feel . . . so you have a drag. I did. Then I wished I hadn't. I told mum, and she said, Don't start. When you go t'youth you see a lot smoking, but they do it to be big, mainly.'

Then they can't stop. In our class there's more than ten smoke now, more girls than boys.'

By this time the doors had opened, and loud music drifted from the building. 'C'mon, let's go in.' Tall boys with the distinctive 'bristle' haircut (crew-cut on top, long and swept back at the sides) blocked the doorway; younger girls squeezed past; a sixteen-year-old in yet another Coat leaned sadly by the door because she had been 'banned' for a couple of weeks for bad behaviour. She stayed there all evening in the cold wind.

Melanie rushed into the girls' cloakroom, careful to introduce Debbie to her schoolfriends, and after another desperate look at her reflection braved the large main hall, where isolated girls bobbed up and down within their own space. To her relief, at least eight of them wore ties.

There was no sign of organized disco dancing. When Melanie rose to dance, completely on her own, she put her hands in the pockets of her skirt, kept her back straight, and swivelled her feet so that she moved about with a curious rolling motion. One or two groups of girls danced in the same way but in lines. When a group of older boys took to the floor the girls scattered. The lads stood in a circle, feet glued to the spot, and tore at the strings of imaginary guitars, flinging their heads dizzily up and down in time to the music. From the seats around the room the others watched, not smiling at the bizarre ritual dance, but appreciating the sheer stamina of the performance. Girls lit cigarettes, and tried each other's coats on. Debbie had seen a girl from Thurnscoe and borrowed a brown version of The Coat for a few moments. Would she like one? 'Well, me mum's on social security so she couldn't afford to get me one. I'm not bothered.'

Outside the room, the youth leaders – Colin and Sandra Roberts-Benton – were preparing a 'pie and peas' supper in the small kitchen, because it was the night before the bonfire night. There was a noise of clanging and shouting from the boys clustered around the table and a constant stream of kids in and out of the doors. Some of the boys looked about twenty; the lower age was technically fourteen. But Sandra explained that they had to turn a blind eye to members like Melanie: 'We have to let them in at thirteen. They're growing up so quickly that they don't want to go to the junior club at that age. Really, the needs of this age group haven't been catered for. We don't really know what to do for them, what they want. Of course they would have the disco every night, but we have games evenings to try to give variety.'

Her husband added: 'They're great kids. They tend to be anti-authority, and since so many of them end up on the dole, they come here and teach the younger ones all the fiddles. But there is nothing for them and it's *not* their fault. Oh, they get into fights – bad fights – but there's no kids more generous when it comes to collecting for charity. There is so much *good* in them, but the public does not see it.'

Melanie – who loved to read Enid Blyton books rather than teenage magazines in the little room with 'Melanie' on the door; who wanted to be sixteen yet had only once had a 'boyfriend' and that for only three weeks; who loved clothes and games with roughly equal intensity; who talked of being a model in London yet got homesick if she was more than one night away from her parents – danced with her curly head flung back, dazzled by the disco lights. She imagined she was a 'Young Generation' dancer, trim and glossy and watched by an audience of thousands. Debbie watched her, too shy to dance herself. And one or two boys, including her friend David, watched her, too, with the beginnings of a fixed admiration, as the scarlet lights turned to blue, and red, and blue.

At home her mother and father sat by the fire, having decided not to go up to Eric's golf club for a drink. 'It's funny,' laughed Pat. 'Up there they've all got big cars, and we park our old motor bike beside them. But they don't mind – Eric can teach them anything about golf.'

He shifted modestly in his chair; in the front room his sports trophies lined the shelves. Eric said he had no worries about his daughter – and his wife added, 'As far as Eric's concerned our Melanie can do no wrong.'

'Well, I'm not worried. Girls, they get married, after a couple of years at work. In this area they go into factories or shops, get about £40 a week. I've got a friend, kept his daughter at school. She got A-levels and went to college, and she got married last week. It's a waste of time, with all that expense. Of course I'd like her to do well at school. But. . . .'

Pat said 'I don't think she'll be clever enough to stay on at school. If she wants to she can.'

Eric stared at the flames, his arms folded. 'I want both my kids to be happy, but I want them to get away from here, see a bit of the world. To this day I regret not going in the army. We're trying to encourage Stephen to try the merchant navy now, I want him to, me. I've seen enough in my time of hard work. I think you want to see the world – not just coal faces, bad health, shifts at terrible hours, dirt. Once you get married you get grooved into this area. In this area you stay down the pits all your life. You're a close-knit community with all the good and bad things of that. If the pits shut up tomorrow, all t'shops would close and Goldthorpe would be a ghost town. There's nothing here. . . . If our Stephen stays down pit he'll see nothing of life. If our Melanie stays round here she'll see nothing. I only hope she'll marry someone as pleasant as herself — not a miner. Definitely not. No, no, no, no, no.' He shook his head.

Pat smiled wryly at him, 'Well, I married you.'

'Yes — well, happiness is the main thing. We've always been thankful for small mercies, always had a holiday each year. But it's the way of life. I'd like our Melanie to move away from the area and try a different way of life, even though we'd miss her. In the morning she gets up singing. She comes home from school and calls, 'Hey up'. She tells us everything — everything that happens at school. When we go on holiday she'll join in races, and get up and dance with us. Our Melanie will never be a worry to us. But she and Stephen would have a better life away from here. And I want to be able to stay with them for holidays.' He looked up and grinned, 'Mind, when my kids go I'll probably cry me eyes out. But it will be better for *them*.'

Winter

10 Rajesh

Rajesh Attra arrived in Leicester five years ago, when he was nine. After twenty six years driving steam trains across the vast spaces of Kenya, his father had retired, and – with his £4000 golden handshake, and considerable savings – decided to 'seek a better future for my family'. Mr Attra came first, to find somewhere to live. Then one November morning Rajesh alighted at Heathrow with his mother, his older brother Balraj and his big sisters Ruprani and Anita. He looked at the grey sky and felt, for the first time, cold.

'Where we lived, in Nairobi, it was hot nearly all the year round, apart from when the rains came. Then it was *quite* cold. When it rained the roads used to go all splodgy, and the hail was this size' – his finger and thumb form a circle – so that when they fell on the tin roofs you could hear them planging like someone throwing stones on the top. I loved it there; it was brilliant – that's all I can say: brilliant. We could always enjoy ourselves, and had money in the bank, and all that. We lived in a bungalow with a big back garden and many flowers. And there were these fruits called Victorias which had a round seed inside with all this, like, syrup, in it. They didn't *put* it in – it was natural. So we could eat a variety of foods like that. Our house was pretty big; and we had a servant, only we didn't treat him like a servant – he was like a member of the family. He was African. We don't like that sort of thing: telling one person to do everything. That's why mum can cook and do all that, because she never minded doing it.

'My dad had all his family in England by then, and they said it was a good place – quiet and reasonable. So my dad said, OK, we'll try, because in Africa he said that there was no future because the Africans were getting violent and causing trouble for us Asians. Uganda was a bad thing. But a year before we came here we went to India for a holiday to see what it was like. It was brilliant – but too hot. You wouldn't have recognized me; I was all brown. I'm dead white now.

'Then dad decided to come to England. At first I was quite glad, because of all the stories I'd heard about England. Like it snowed a lot, and we'd never seen snow before. So I was quite glad to come. My dad and my uncle met us at the airport, and we came here – to Leicester. Dad had found a place to live – not this house, another one. We rented it – in the Highfields area. That was for that first winter, when it was so cold. But we didn't like it round there – there was too much trouble. Like people would come out of the pub at night and shout and smash bottles, and there were lots of bad people round there. So my dad says, We have to find a house. So we looked around and found this one. My dad and my brother painted it, and we got furniture quite slowly, and did it all ourselves. And so we've been living here ever since. But then I came not to like this country as much. I realized that our life in Kenya was so much better.'

Rajesh is small for his age and describes himself as 'a bit too fat'. His face is round and serious; his smile when it appears is oddly lopsided, as if he were embarrassed at the sensitive pleasure it reveals. He lives with his family in a thirties semi-detached house, in a quiet road of identical houses, situated in a relatively prosperous area of Leicester. Five years ago the house – comfortable, with four bedrooms, central heating, and a new three-piece suite in the best front room – cost £9000. Rajesh's father is pleased that it is now worth far more, that the early struggle to buy and furnish it has paid off. Despite his ill health after a heart attack a year ago, Mr Attra works as a skilled machine operator in a factory. He still misses his railways, and goes once a week to a railway enthusiasts' club to reminisce about the great days of steam.

Mrs Attra, a beautiful woman who wears rustling saris under a Marks and Spencer cardigan, works as a nursing assistant in the General Hospital – 'Helping the nurses and the patients and doing everything.' Her oldest son, who is now twenty, commutes every day to London where he works as a trainee accountant with a firm of jewellers. He tried living away but, despite his neo-cockney accent, expensive fashionable clothes and confident air, Balraj found that he missed the closeness of his family.

Morning in their house is busy – with Balraj rushing to catch his London train, Mr and Mrs Attra making breakfast before leaving for work, and Anita rising early to revise for her O-levels. Rajesh himself gets up at 6 a.m., does his exercises to keep fit, eats his breakfast, then does homework or revision until 7.25 when he leaves to catch the 67 bus to school. Each morning basketball practice starts at 8 a.m. at Judgemeadow Comprehensive, and Rajesh, though he is far from the best in the team, is keen to improve. He was surprised and pleased even to be chosen, which is why the hour's extra 'school' does not worry him. His worst problem is tiredness; so anxious is Rajesh to improve his written English and do well at school that he rarely goes to bed before 11.30 at night.

While Judgemeadow School was being built in 1972 General Amin's racist policies started to drive many Asians to England, and especially to Leicester, to swell the existing Asian community. The pressure for school places meant that the school had to open before it was properly finished, with only 300 pupils, a high staff turnover and a streaming system. There was great opposition from people who lived in the £30,000 modern houses on the estate facing Judgemeadow, who objected to 'that black school'.

Judgemeadow now has 1200 pupils, from a catchment area which includes Highfields, notorious for its poor housing, shifting population, and considerable social problems, but which also embraces white middle-class areas. So Judgemeadow's headmaster Anthony Green is proud of the fact that the school contains 'a complete social range' amongst its fifteen mother-tongue languages. Sixty-five per cent of the pupils are West Indian or Asian – a fact which no longer worries the people in the smart houses across the road (which are not, oddly enough, in Mr Green's catchment area). The school has a good reputation, and local residents even collected money to donate young trees to the grounds. The school motto is 'Fraternity', and Anthony Green asserts, 'Our school culture is what unifies the children.'

Judgemeadow is no longer streamed, nor does it have a conventional remedial department. Anthony Green believes that a child who is very good at woodwork could be in a top set for that subject, though he may need remedial English. He calls it a 'child-based structure', which means that Rajesh, for example, is with different groups of children for most subjects. It seems a complicated system, but the children seem to cope – Rajesh joining Hitesh and Hitendra and Dinesh for English, then perhaps leaving them whilst they take French and he takes extra English, then meeting up with Hitendra for biology, and so on through the day, without worrying about the fragmentation.

The school is light and open-plan; three history lessons could be going on in one 'area', with an almost perpetual noise and movement which is distracting for the outsider. The school, though beautiful with excellent facilities, appears too small for all its children. Or perhaps the individual child seems too small for the school. It would be impossible for a headmaster to know 1200 pupils well; so it is not surprising that the headmaster does not really know Rajesh Attra. Even the year tutor says, 'I don't really know Rajesh. Unfortunately I only tend to get to know the ones with the problems.'

Rajesh has no problems. He sits in the front row of his history lesson, next to Hitendra (his closest friend) and listens to Mr Pendergast's stories of the Great Plague. As in most of his lessons it is the girls who are the noisy and boisterous ones — extremely pretty Asian girls with long black hair, one of them wearing a red bomber jacket over her blue uniform. Four of them are whispering about 'Grease', and arguing whether John Travolta really is handsome or not. But even they are diverted by the tales of swellings under arms and bodies dumped in pits, and a catalogue of causes of death in seventeenth-century England. They grimace. Beyond the large windows silvery frost still lies in large patches on the grass, where the brilliant sunlight has not reached. One or two of the children stare out. Their school stands in 18 acres at the edge of Leicester; behind it, rolling farmland stretches towards trees and a distant spire. It is very different from the narrow streets of Highfields where many of them live.

Mr Pendergast demands attention. 'Now some of you are going to want to take history next year. Some of you won't. But don't think: If I study history it won't help me get a job, because that's nonsense. If you take history and go for a job your employer will ask you how many O-levels you got — he won't ask you what they were. If you've got history it's as good as any. And when you do history in the fifth year you'll study world problems, like Vietnam and the Middle East and the problems in Africa. It increases your understanding of the world, and at your age that's what you have to start thinking about. So remember that when you make your choices. . . .' As always Rajesh hunches over his desk, staring seriously at the teacher. In lessons he rarely smiles or talks.

In history, as in all other lessons, Rajesh sits with other Asian boys. The rest of the children divide similarly, with West Indian girls sitting together and English boys sauntering into the room in a little group. It is not that they display any animosity to each other; quite the reverse. Rajesh says, 'All my class are my friends.' But occasionally in a particular lesson he will speak Punjabi to his neighbour, and in a biology lesson he and his friends do not share the ribaldry of the rest. Mrs Stuart (who shows by her good humour that she really likes the children) is telling them about the human skeleton. The girls shudder and giggle as she takes a life-size skeleton from the cupboard and holds it, yellow and gangling, up for them to see. They discuss the skull. 'Now what do you know about it? Is it a joint like the other parts we've listed? . . . That's right, Paul. The skull has a soft spot in the middle. This is because a baby has to come through here, the pelvic girdle, and out through the vagina. Now vaginas aren't very big, so the baby has a soft skull with some give in it . . . otherwise it would be pretty agonising.'

Two West Indian girls are nudging and laughing aloud; most of the girls smile; and the white boys in the class look sideways at each other with broad grins. The Asian girls share the joke; most of the Asian boys look uncomfortable. Rajesh and his little group of friends look straight down at their hands, embarrassed. Then one of the West Indian girls calls out, 'Hey, miss, are we doing reproduction next week?'

Mrs Stuart laughs: 'No, we're doing muscles – but you may hope!'

Throughout the days, from lesson to lesson, Rajesh is reminded of what is expected. In mathematics: 'Some of you are going to pay dearly for your neatness – or lack of it. When it comes to exams in the fifth year the examiner will simply put a line through and give you zero if he can't read what you have put – so remember it and start working to improve your writing.'

In English: 'Don't worry if I seem to have given you a low mark for your homework. It's silly me giving you twenty out of thirty, if in an examination another member of the department is going to give you ten out of thirty. So if I've given you twelve out of thirty for your story, don't worry. There's plenty of others going to get less than this group, I can tell you.'

In biology: 'It's your exam next week, and this is what's in it – everything we've done on respiration and everything we've done on excretion. Don't forget the kidneys. . . . Hey, listen at the back! I'm telling you this for *your* benefit, not mine!'

Rajesh responds to the pressure. He wants to do well. 'Five years in this country seems a long time, but it isn't. Like – my English is not that good. Not as good as my big brother's anyway. He's as clever as everything, and so is Anita, but I'm not so clever as them. Like spelling. I'm really poor at spelling; flat out – I can't spell much at all. So I have extra English lessons. I've changed this year – because my sister told me that this is the hardest year if you want to do any O-levels. You have to work. Like last year, I used to finish me homework and watch telly. She told me not to, but I didn't listen to her much. I used to talk in class and be jolly. They put you in groups going on what marks you got. . . . Some of my friends – well, I don't call them friends because they act big-headed because they're in the top groups from me – they've been here a long time, they're good in English and they're clever. They say, Oh, he can't spell this; Oh, he can't spell that; Oh, he's dumb; Oh, he's this and that. . . .' If they got dropped down a group and someone teased them they wouldn't like it at all. I may not be clever, but at least I try.

'In Africa I could be top, you see. I used to get As, As, As, As, As, As. It was a little school – yes – and we spoke English. When I went to this school my report wasn't that good for the first few times, but it's getting better. Last time it was as good a standard as the rest. I was pleased with myself. I wasn't used to none of this studying, and I'm just catching on now. My big brother did brilliantly, and both my sisters got As. So every year I try to catch up. Eventually I'm trying to beat Anita! So this year I don't talk much.

'I think competition helps you a lot. Like one of my friends – last year he didn't work but this year he's pulled his socks up because he doesn't want to be left behind. And he gets good marks now. Last year I used to beat him; this year he beats me. So I always try as hard as I can to get in front of him, even though he is beating me by little marks. But we're good friends. I tell you the thing I hate about people – that if they are good they show off about it. Why? If *they* know it, that's enough. But if I was top of the class . . . I *might* . . . want to show off about it. Say: Oh yes, I get good marks, and things like that. But you always have to remember what other people are thinking. I'd like to be in the top groups. If I had a wish, first of all I'd make myself clever. That's one thing I'd love to do. Then my other friends who are not clever as well – because sometimes they can't do things and if you ask the teacher two or three times, they get annoyed with you. They criticize, and when they do that you don't feel like going on with the work, you feel like getting your own back. Then, when I was clever, I'd *show* them for sure. I'd be a scientist . . . but I don't think I'd be able to do that. Or I'd own a garage. I'd love to work in that trade. It depends. Hard work is very tiring, I know that much. I'd like to be so clever that I could do all my work immediately. Last night I went to bed early for me – half past eleven. Usually it's twelve, and once it was one o'clock.'

On Wednesday morning Rajesh has a double lesson of religious instruction; 'I like RE. I can honestly say it is one of my best subjects. Last year I got a very good mark in RE.' In the first year at Judgemeadow the pupils have a general introduction to all the religions practised by the pupils at the school: Christianity, Islam, Hinduism, Sikhism and Judaism. The second year is devoted to a study of Christianity, with its various denominations, and thereafter detailed comparative religion is taught. In Rajesh's class that morning two of the white children do not take part in the lesson. Their parents object to them learning about Asian religions, and so they sit amongst the rest doing homework, occasionally looking up to listen.

The morning's lesson is about the way of life of the Sikh family. The teacher, Mrs Wood, plays them a recorded interview with a Sikh, in which he explains why he wears a turban, what he believes, what happens at his religious ceremonies. The question-answer format was broken occasionally by Indian music – causing one or two of the white children to grin at each other, and the girl who is 'opted-out' to nudge a neighbour, who covers her mouth with her hand. The two Sikh boys in the class stare straight ahead, as if embarrassed slightly by the revelation of their culture. Rajesh sits in the back corner of the room, silhouetted against the bright cold sunlight streaming in at the windows. When Mrs Wood hands round a discussion paper about Sikh customs he studies it carefully.

One of the questions on the paper concerns arranged marriages. Three months earlier Rajesh's elegant nineteen-year-old sister, Ruprani, married after a two-week courtship. Her father and mother had chosen the groom, the son of acquaintances. The couple met, went out together, and agreed to the marriage – whereupon Mr Attra gave expensive presents to the groom and all his family, as well as settling some capital upon his daughter. It is (he had explained the night before) the custom amongst Asians to give such dowries: 'It is too much, too much money for me. But we have to do it or people will talk about girl, and boy's family will not be pleased.'

Mrs Attra had proudly shown photographs of the beautiful bride with her handsome groom, garlanded for their wedding. Ruprani herself was staying at home whilst her husband looked for work and accommodation in London but talked excitedly to him on the telephone each night. She said she was very happy to be married.

In class the subject causes a flurry of interest. Mrs Wood asks for someone to speak against arranged marriages, and four or five girls put up their hands. First to speak is Melanie, a tall, confident West

Indian girl: 'Why should you have to marry somebody you don't know? How can you tell you love him if you've hardly met him?'

The teacher asks for someone to defend arranged marriages, adding, as his hand shoots up, 'I thought you'd have something to say, Rajesh.'

He speaks loudly: 'The girl doesn't *have* to marry the boy, miss. She can have two weeks to get to know him, and then if she doesn't want to marry him she can say so.'

The English and West Indian girls make derisive noises: 'Oh, how can she tell what he's like after two weeks? He might be nice to her and then batter her once they are married. It's stupid, that's all it is — *stupid*.'

The Sikh who is sitting next to Rajesh puts up his hand: 'She doesn't *have* to marry the boy, miss,' he repeats, almost sullenly.

'So you agree with Rajesh . . . well, this is a subject which always rouses strong feelings. We could go on discussing it all lesson, but let's move on to the next question. . . .'

That night Rajesh said: 'I'm really proud of my religion. I would like to see it the top religion. You know some people have to go to church every Sunday? Well, we can worship our God in our hearts — here at home.' He puts his hand on his breast. 'I am proud of being an Indian. There's every type of religion in the world, but I think Hinduism is the oldest. Like, in Christianity they say, Right, *this* is the only way, and they worship their own god. But in our religion we say there are many societies trying to reach God, and you don't have to go one way, you can go a different way. So there are different types inside our religion. And all the time you're learning, you're learning to go onwards to God. God — you don't know who God is. You see all the statues in the temples and the super one of all the gods is Brahman. He is the sort of supervisor of the gods. But at the very top of the temple, they won't have another statue there. Because we don't know who God is. You *can't* know who he is. But all the other gods help you, because every time you learn about them you've climbed up a ladder to the real true God. Getting closer to God. . . . So really it doesn't matter which God you worship. We don't think it matters, as long as you do good deed so that you can be closer to God.

'In school we learn about all the religions. But I don't know if English people think our religion is as good as their religion. You see, we have Diwali in October, and we have candles around the house, and presents and fireworks. It is like your New Year. We celebrate Christmas as well. Me and my sister will decorate a Christmas tree and buy some presents. But one thing I don't like is: *we* don't get a holiday for Diwali. Like, the majority is English, and they can get a holiday for Christmas. But if they can get that, why can't we get a holiday for Diwali? This year we were lucky because it came in our half-term holiday. But otherwise we have to come to school, and yet people don't have to go to school at Christmas. . . . But this year it was all right. We had plenty of fireworks in our garden, and this year was the best Diwali I've ever had in this country.'

At six promptly – as he does every evening, believing firmly in routine – Rajesh went to do his homework. He and Anita work on the dining table in the back room, where their grandmother lay sick in bed. Mr Attra's mother, who bore twenty children in Kenya, came to England before her oldest son, but now lives with him. 'My mother cannot stand the cold,' explained Mr Attra, as he flopped into one of the large striped armchairs in the front room and lit a cigarette. 'So she has been ill for a while. No, she does not speak English, although she can go to the shops and come back with the right things. The children speak some English to her so she is learning small words. They speak Punjabi to each other sometimes, and sometimes English.'

Mrs Attra talked about her children, apologizing for her own slightly halting English: 'We are glad they are doing well . . . all of them. Rajesh works hard at school. He looks like a little boy but he thinks like an old man. You know you quarrel with your husband? Everybody does. He push me into the kitchen and say, Mummy, mummy, no, please, don't. And he goes to my husband and says, No, daddy, don't say that. And he comes back to me and say, Are you all right now, mummy? He's funny like that. And he wants to hear stories all the time. He sits with his grandmother and asks her stories about the old days, and she tells him, and I wonder how he got interested in stories like that. A young boy. . . . Sometimes I wonder what he is, you know, thinking in his head?'

Rajesh thinks a lot. He thinks that in many ways he is lucky – loving and being loved by his family, having a comfortable home with plenty of pocket money, going to a really good school where he has lots of friends. But he also thinks that in a complicated, nebulous way, life is difficult.

He sat upright in the armchair, gesticulating wildly, trying to explain: 'I know I am British because my dad had a British passport and I came here on his passport. In some ways I would like to think of myself as British, but in some ways not. Why? Because I'm born African, simple as that. I love Africa still. Think it's the best place in the world — even though the Africans didn't want us there. But now I'm ambitious to go to Sweden because — one thing — Indians don't go there. See ... like ... you could say that people think Indians are very low. Think they make themselves low. Now in Sweden there's not a lot of Indians. There's not colour prejudice. When you meet one person who's different you'd obviously got to like him. But as soon as other people come, lots of them, the people say, Oh, Indian people do that, and then others hear about it and say, Oh, we don't want these people coming to our country. And they don't like the people who are different any more.

'Like, my sister, she's qualified, and yet she can't get a job. She works training for computers (I don't know what she does), but she wants to go to London and find a job. But now there's so many English people that don't go to work that the Indians can get back, because now there are Indians that own the factories and all. So now an English person could go there for a job, and they say no. It's like a war.' He shakes his head sadly. 'Like, if they *both* stopped the colour prejudice everyone could be working happily. That's probably why I'd like to go to Sweden. It sounds a good place. Like when I came to England it sounded a good place.

'No, I don't think it's a *bad* place. It's just what part you're in. If you've been to a part like Skegness, for a day trip, it's lovely. We went for a day trip and everyone was friendly. You know, they aren't used to having Indians, and they didn't sort of go, 'Oh, who are *these*?' They were *friendly*. If you went to Scotland everyone would be friendly, or to Wales. But if you go to London ... well, there are a lot of Indians there and people don't like them. So there are lots of people causing trouble.

'Like, there is this National Front. I know what it is. I think it's plain stupid, I really do. They say — the people coming from Uganda, we don't want them here. Why not? Simple as that — why not? They say they're different coloured. Well, my dad took sweat working for paying our tickets to come here, and he works hard for us now. We all do. Refugees? So what, if they come here and work? Like, some of us Indian people are very nice, and some West Indian people are very nice, too. But *they* cause a big problem — the National Front. Like, there's this kid I know at school. He may be tough, but I think he's mad — showing off. He wears a leather jacket, and I think he carries a chain with him. It's best to keep your mouth closed, even if you know the thing – it's best to keep your mouth closed. Anyway, that kid goes round talking about 'Pakis' and things like that. Just wants to act big. So what if he's got a chain? Some day someone's going to be better than him and carry a knife. If they do, he won't touch his chain again. . . .

'There's this Indian kid at school. He should be proud of being Indian but him – he's had his hair all curled up, and if you talk to him in Punjabi or Gujarati he'll swear at you. He's pretending to be English. Pretending to be one of the big bullies. If you say something to him about India he'll say, You shut your gob. He's ashamed. Like me – you can say, why aren't I ashamed? Because I'm proud of myself – proud of being Indian. He could be the same, but he doesn't want to. See, I have English friends . . . but if you have only English friends and they're bullies and you really go into their friendship – you know, you go like them, you turn into one of those bullies and be ashamed to be Indian. If you mix with everyone you're on the level. You go with your English friends and you go with your Indian friends as well. It's just like a balance with weights on it. You're in the middle, and you've got weights on both sides. If you're balanced, and you see fighting, you're in the middle. You don't fight too much, and you don't make peace too much, because if you make peace too much you'll get picked on. Like one of my friends – he isn't tough at all. If someone hits him, he'd just take it. But though I don't like fighting, I'd go after him. You have to. It's an important fact of life.

'See – I'm not sure people here welcome people like me. Not really – to tell the truth. Because like in school, you see the English kids and the West Indian or Jamaican kids – so they're tough – so what, if we're peaceful? Why go ahead and bully them, if they bully us? Sometimes they shame the school – and it's a *good* school. They write on the walls; the toilets were closed because someone broke a pipe off; a whole toilet was broken because they threw bricks at it. And those boys, sometimes they say, Give me 10p, and a kid might say, I've only got the right amount for my dinner, but if they aren't strong they'd give the money. Then if you're standing there just doing nothing they'd say, Get out of the way, and if you say no they'll boot you.

'I'd say they do pick on us, because the Indians don't like fighting at all. But there is one or two Indians that are tough and they get their own back. Like there's a gang in Leicester – it's an Indian gang, and they find out if some Indian kids gets a beating, very badly – they'd get revenge. I don't know if that's a good thing. It could be and it couldn't be. Because if they do that it could carry on and on. But if they don't the others would take advantage and say, They don't even hit back so we can do it.

'To get somewhere you have to do something you don't want to. Like there used to be a boy in class − a white boy − who was a troublemaker. But at first he was good − not a bully. He even used to go to another friend's house, an Indian house, have a meal there, and play with Indian children. He was a friend then, and we used to laugh. But then we went through the first year at school, and he caught on to English people − and then he started to call Indian people 'Pakis' and that. Say they stink, and all this. Now I think he hates them. . . . No, I don't think he *really* does, but see − you've got a sort of responsibility: what's expected of you by your friends. That's how he is.

'It just comes along in life. Like a friend of mine, and he didn't used to fight at all, but I taught him to fight and he's tougher than me now. We go round together: we play but we can punch hard. So it's really like that. You don't feel pain . . . or, you do feel it, but then you want to get that person back. So it develops your insight: to be stronger on the outside makes a shell for you. Inside you may be soft, but you've got an outer shell. Like some people are all hard outside, but you can never know what is inside.

'This year some of us went youth hostelling. One of our teachers took a small group of us, and I wanted to go because, see, Indians don't go out much. See, they're not recognized. They do everything in their own race. But they don't go out and mix with other people, and so we said that for a change we would. I persuaded my friends. Because birds should not always go together to the same place. Why not try? So we discussed it, and we thought it would be good. We thought that everybody would be friendly. But we went out there [to the hostels] and you know, people give you the looks. The minute you walk in there they give you the looks. You know, like, they're not saying it, but you can figure it out from the looks: Oh God, where do *they* come from? and all this. We knew it would happen. But it sort of puts you off. You've walked all this way with your pack and they don't want you around. But then, after a while, when they got used to us it was OK. In the end some turned out to be really friendly. It *could* make you angry − those looks − but I wouldn't like to see that day.

'I would honestly say I am a happy person. If my mum tells me to do something, and I say no, and she asks me again and says please, then I'll get up. Anything they ask me, any of my family, I always do it – I don't know why. Even if I don't want to do it, even if outside it's cold and freezing like it is now – it's just inside me. My body just doesn't say no, and that's that. But it worries me – the thought of getting in a temper. I've been doing so much, and I'm so tired, and somebody asks me to do more – and I'm afraid my temperature could bust completely. Really the anger that builds up inside me from everything, usually comes out at home. . . .'

(BM: 'When did you first think that violence is a part of life?')

'About when I came to this country, when I was nine. See – first we came here: everyone was good. But as . . . well, at first I didn't think I would ever fight, not in a million. But as the kids get older, they start. It's like a competition; they say, Who is the best, and you say, I am, and that's how fighting sort of begins. You change from when you're little. First there is a bridge to other people, when you are very young. You know, when you're sort of small you want to be friendly to everybody. It goes up to about . . . eight, let's say. Then they sort of start changing. Then you see all the fights going on, and it works its way up, it gradually builds inside you as you get older. If you get it in you that you don't like people then you have fight after fight after fight, until you start to realize that it's not right, this fighting. There's this period when you want to be toughest, you want to be best. That lasts to about sixteen, or it can even to on until eighteen. After that perhaps the friendly period comes again. But in between . . . well, I've told you four or five times that I don't like fighting. I can't say it enough. But I *have* to. See, as you get older, something happens to your mind.'

11 Wendy

'I'm very quiet – shy. I'm often shy with people my own age who are different to me – until perhaps I get to know them. I'm not too shy with grown-ups as long as I don't know them and they don't know me. I like meeting somebody new. Yes, I suppose it's because I am afraid of what some people think of me – when I get to know them. Occasionally, that is. It's . . . what they might say to other people, you know? Sometimes things that aren't true. Some people are jealous – if one does well. But I don't honestly mind. I used to be terribly shy with everyone, but I'm not any more. I try not to draw attention to myself at all. I just enjoy learning. . . . Yes, I think you could say I'm typical of the girls at my school. Just typical.'

Wendy Moor is fifteen years old. She is in her O-level year as a day girl at St Felix School, which stands in acres of smooth playing fields and marshy land, just outside the prosperous little town of Southwold on the east coast of England. A bitter east wind whistles around the cluster of beautifully proportioned neo-Georgian buildings, causing the fir trees to creak and groan. St Felix was founded in 1897 and named after the patron saint of East Anglia. The first headmistress chose *Felix quia Fortis* as motto of the institution which would apotheosise her life's ambition: 'to found a school where girls can be treated as sensible beings'. In the twenties, when science was not thought a fit subject for young ladies, the second headmistress founded a well-equipped science block. Today the new headmistress (though a classicist herself) encourages as many girls as possible to take sciences and even engineering at university. The school honours boards in the hall record successes at Oxford and Cambridge, as well as at other universities. With its swimming pool, new squash courts, music wing, comfortable furnished 'Houses' for the boarders, library with valuable first editions on its shelves, and an ethos based proudly upon competition, St Felix has an atmosphere which does not contradict its motto. It is an atmosphere which Wendy has absorbed.

'I was born in Norwich, and we lived then where we live now, near Beccles. I went to a private nursery school in Ditchingham –

only about twelve people there constantly. It was just down the road from All Hallows, which is a large convent school, with junior and senior schools. The junior was very, very good. So I was at the nursery till I was seven, and at All Hallows till I was eleven. I loved it there. Very happy. Everyone was so friendly. There were only about fifty of us. But the senior school didn't have very many facilities so my parents wanted me to move.

Well, I took three school exams in the end. I tried for a scholarship to Roedean. I had to stay for three days actually there. I was very frightened because it was an enormous school right by the sea. Scared *stiff*! I didn't get the scholarship. I'd been put down for St Felix, so I took that exam and I took one for All Hallows senior school. I was one of the people chosen to come and have an interview at St Felix. I had a half day here, and an intelligence test. We were interviewed by each of the heads of department, and then by the old headmistress as well. Her study seemed enormous. The old table and chairs and everything. Sit down there, she says, and she points you to a big armchair! We got a letter saying I'd got a scholarship. I was very happy and my parents were very pleased. I felt I wanted to go somewhere where I could make the best of things. I just wanted to do my best. . . . For . . . my parents, I suppose. I suppose I just wanted to learn more about the world and everybody – and do my best. When I came to the school I thought I would like it here. It seemed a free place. Everybody seemed very happy.

'I don't think my parents felt that state education is very good. Say – discipline-wise, and things like that. I don't think you can learn, because there are a lot of people at those schools who can't be bothered, and so the people who want to learn can't, you see. It doesn't seem right. No point in having a school at all, really. Seems a waste of everybody's money. Discipline is good at our school, but it's not sort of forced on you. You're still very happy, and everybody's free, you know. You wouldn't *want* to misbehave. It's to do with . . . sort of . . . *manners*. Politeness. At our school everybody's terribly aware of each other. I'm not sure that in state schools people aren't impolite. Obviously we have *some* people who aren't considerate, but most are. Most of the girls are boarders and they seem to like it. The standard of teaching is very high, I think. . . . Yes, my parents have struggled, I think. My sister goes to St Felix and my little brother goes to a prep school, so it must be very expensive. I think they want the best for us – so that we can know more things and be better equipped for future life, I suppose.'

A December morning: cold sun pale gold through the deep windows of the school hall. Teachers sit on the polished window seats; in front of them 360 Felicians sit cross-legged in straight rows, under the curved roof. On the platform the headmistress, Mrs Anne Mustoe, wearing a black academic robe, sits in front of the school executive: members of the sixth form dressed in 'mufti' – their own clothes. At the back of the hall the choir stands on a raised dais – and amongst them is Wendy. This is the scene she sees each weekday morning: the rows of heads with hair cropped or tied back, the gold jerseys and green pinafores, the beautifully draped proscenium arch, and the whole school together, singing.

Once a week, a different form takes assembly; this particular morning it is the turn of Lower V. Two small girls stand next to Mrs Mustoe, looking nervously at the pink blur of faces before them. One of them announces: 'This morning's theme is children, and we're going to play you a record.' The girls shuffle in anticipation. A pause; an amplified hiss – then a repetitive catchy tune fills the hall, with a bright young man's voice singing:

> 'We gotta make children happy,
> Oh, we gotta make children happy. . . .'

It goes on a long time. The staff look ahead, faintly amused, perhaps slightly bored.

When it is finished, the two girls on the stage read the prayers in their high, self conscious voices:

'Oh God, our Heavenly Father, we remember before you all destitute and sorrowful children: those whose homes have been destroyed by war; those living in camps for whom family life has no meaning; those without knowledge of their parents; those who have suffered years of terror and persecution; all who are sick with loneliness or suffering from bodily disease. Make our hearts burn within us for the children of the dark places of the world. . . .'

Then:

'Dear Father, we pray that you will help those children in other countries who do not have the opportunities we have. We ask you to give them the skill to read and write and the spirit to use their skill for the good of mankind. . . .'

Wendy's head is bowed, like those of her neighbours. She listens to the prayers, and wonders, with a slight and passing feeling of helplessness, what can be done.

'If people are actually listening to the prayers, and not thinking of something else, it can have an effect on them. It can make you think. When we have readings in assembly I do think about them. Very often I forget, but then sometimes afterwards I think about it and it has an impression on me. When I've never thought of something before. Like ... children in countries where, you know, they're starving, and everything. I feel ever so sorry for them. And I can imagine what it must be like to have a broken home. There are quite a lot of girls at school with divorced parents. Surprising. They don't talk about it. Sometimes they're very unhappy. You can see they are, but they wouldn't talk about it in public, as it were. You just gradually come to know that they go to so-and-so for these holidays, then to so-and-so for those holidays. Or they say, I'm going out with my father this weekend, and you think, Why just your father? And you know the parents are divorced. You don't notice when you're little.

'I wasn't aware of things like that when I was young. I mean, I'm secure, and I'm getting a good education, and I've a good home and ... just, you know, rather fortunate. But still, you start thinking about things when you reach the age of about twelve or thirteen. You start really thinking. Er ... there's an awful lot of unhappiness, isn't there? In the moments when I stop working I think about all the different parts of the country and all the places I've visited, and that's nice. But when you see the news, you know, you think about that certain country which you wouldn't otherwise think about. There are some countries which are very unhappy. Fighting. . . . It depresses me, it does. And that thing when they were going to kill all the baby seals. Things like that. People quarrelling all the time. It does depress me. I don't say it doesn't matter because it's nothing to do with me, it really depresses me. It's amazing to think that people can be so horrid. Just going around killing seems so ... *ridiculous*. And you think of another war ... terrifying. I suppose these days they would just drop an atom bomb and the whole world would just blow up.'

There are twenty girls in the class, sitting at single, new, Formica tables a couple of feet apart. Wendy sits at the back, a pile of books before her. She whispers to a neighbour. The rest of the class is boisterously noisy, quietening only a little when their small, energetic Latin teacher sweeps into the room.

'Now, girls, today we're carrying on with subjunctives. . . .' They groan loudly. Briskly, the teacher scribbles fifteen or so sentences on the board for them to translate from Latin to English. They groan again, with the air of those who enjoy playing at protest.

What's *placidus?*' What's *quis?* What's *intellegere?*' Their teacher does not suggest they consult their dictionaries, but answers each girl quickly, so that the process is not drawn out. 'Now prep. . . .' Loud groans. 'I want you to do page seventy. It is well up to O-level standard, so don't be surprised if you find it hard. . . .' There is a rustling as the girls note down what they must do. The atmosphere is relaxed. One or two of the girls even answer the teacher back, but she shows no sign of growing irritated – simply brisker, so that the first lesson of the double period ends with astonishing speed.

Wendy has already opened her book of selections from Virgil in anticipation of the poetry lesson which always fills the second period. The girls obviously enjoy it – especially as they have reached the story of Dido and Aeneas.

'So they . . . er . . . *shared* the same cave, did they?'

'Yes, you see, they considered themselves married.'

They hoot with derision: 'Oh yes, oh *yes*! We know all about *that*'

The teacher is amused but ironic: 'Virgil takes this very delicately. He hasn't got the same suggestive mind as you!'

'But Dido, she knows it's wrong, doesn't she?'

'And Virgil doesn't tell us what Aeneas thinks about all this.'

They continue reading the Latin and translating aloud, with pauses for comment – and jokes. A long metaphor about Atlas is a source of more merriment: 'But, if Atlas is holding up the world, how can he have children?'

'Oh, Sarah, you really must get over your rationalistic view of things. You have to imagine a world in which every tree and every stream is the personification of a god.'

'I know that, but I was just wondering *how*, if he was holding the world up, *how*. . . .'

Wendy smiles down at her book. there is a chorus of 'Sar-*ah*!' The teacher tries once more, tongue in cheek, to explain about gods. . . .

'Look, I'm happy about him holding the *world* up, but. . . .'

'Is it just the actually having of children that bothers you?'

'Yes.'

Then there is a shout from the back of the room: 'Don't worry, he probably brought in a jack!' Miss Jenkins joins in the laughter. Then Wendy's class continue to read with serious attention the sad tale of Dido's hopes, betrayal and death.

'I feel sorry for people who, you know, really *try* in school, who really struggle a lot. Most of them don't do very well after all the work. I don't feel sorry for people who don't bother to try at all. But most people at my school work hard. I like working hard. . . . It's all to help you later on. It helps you to get on with other people, and things like that – as well as jobs. Like Latin – it helps a lot with French, and helps a lot with everything. I mean, a lot of English words derive from Latin. It helps you to think, too. It's not a waste of time. There's a lot of history behind it as well. They don't teach Latin in comprehensives, do they? I don't see there's any reason why they shouldn't. It's not that it's beyond them, it's just not there for them. I suppose it depends on the type of person you are. Well, if Latin's not going to be any help, because they are not doing French, there *isn't* an awful lot of point to it, I suppose.'

'Are you going to Bilge, Wendy?'

'Yes.'

Wendy scurries through the draughty cloisters and along the suddenly warm corridor to the biology lab. The large windows look over misty marshland, beyond the playing fields. There is a smell of chemicals; a sound of clicks and shouts from the hockey field, and the sweet notes of a distant flute. The girls sit at the high wooden benches, taking down the notes that are dictated at speed. Wendy writes a heading, 'The Nervous System', and underlines it neatly. They learn about 'the simple animal Hydra', and how their own knees shoot up when tapped in a certain place.

'Conditioned reflexes are learned, unconditioned reflexes are not learned. . . .'

The laboratory is well-equipped, including a brand-new microscope to add to the ones already in use. The girls queue to peer down at slides, grotesquely magnified, of tissue.

'The name of the man who did these experiments was called Pavlov. He carried out classic experiments on conditioned reflexes in dogs. This is what he did. . . .'

Wendy writes furiously in her careful handwriting. The girls behind her keep hissing her name, asking to borrow her rubber, her ruler, a pencil, knowing that she, efficient as ever, will have them. Each time they have to draw a diagram they call 'Wendy' again. She grins in mock-exasperation each time, turning to fling the desired object. Towards the end of the lesson, a girl in the front row calls out, 'When can we have our results?' They had taken a mock O-level a week earlier.

'Not yet. I've got them but Mrs Mustoe hasn't seen them yet, so I can't give them to you. You'll have them on Wednesday.'

There is a mumble of groans. The girl in the front row turns round and says to the group behind her: 'It's all right. We know. We *could* have come first, but we didn't want to show Wendy up!' They grin and turn round to where Wendy is sitting, next to the quiet studious girl called Julia who has already decided that she wants to study medicine and then specialize in forensics. They are both bent over their diagram.

The girls in front take up the tease, with a fair degree of mocking aggression: 'Yes, did you hear that, Wendy? We could have come first but we didn't want to show you up. So you needn't worry. . . .' They are forced to face the front frustrated, because Wendy still does not hear. But later that day Wendy learns what they suspect: she has come equal first in her year.

'I've done my English language, English literature and history O-level already. Now I'm doing French, Latin, physics, chemistry, biology, music, maths and additional maths. I'm trying to give up one of them – additional maths. I don't find it interesting and I'm not really mathematical. I've just *got* to give up something. I'm just *too* crammed. This term I've got very tired. When I'm tired I can't concentrate and it doesn't help much. I got As for the first three; but on the other hand they were three of my best subjects. I'll do A-levels, of course, but I haven't really decided which ones.' She sighs.

'The science teachers have sort of been expecting me to do science, because it's always considered . . . you know, if you're clever you do science. But I don't really know if I could cope. It gets so mathematical I don't know if I could manage. So I've been thinking of history and music and possibly English, Latin and French. I don't know.' She heaves another sigh. 'It's so hard to make up one's mind. . . .'

Wendy lives with her parents, brother and sister in a large, open-plan bungalow just outside the little town of Beccles, about fifteen miles from St Felix. David Moor designed the bungalow himself, fifteen years ago, and they moved into it shortly after Wendy was born. The enormous sitting room is crowded, shelf upon shelf, with the Moors' collection of antique glass: twisted sugar-cane patterns in top-hats, shoes and intricate vases. Glass rolling pins, blue and red, hang upon the walls. Modern furniture jostles with beautiful antiques. A fire crackles in the grate. Wendy and her sister Susie, who is thirteen, sit on the sofa, not bothering to change from their uniforms, whilst their little brother Christopher does his prep round the corner in the kitchen. They usually arrive home from school around 6.30 and leave again at 7.50 a.m. the next morning, driven on a rota system.

David and Janet Moor proudly show objects from their collection; their chief pleasure in holidays is to scour antique shops for new additions though they fear now that they may have to sell part of their collection. Wendy would like to collect something, too, but everything is too expensive now, she says, in antiques, that is. Their bungalow is on a hill. Not far away they have a small boat moored on the river – which David Moor is thinking of selling. Wendy used to have a pony, but he was sold because she has so little time to ride.

Wendy's father has a degree in zoology from Oxford and now manages a successful fruit farming co-operative – a job which, with his family background in agriculture, he loves. David and Janet admit that their daughter is right – that to send three children to independent schools is very expensive: 'All our money – or almost all of it – is spent on education. And when you think we've paid for the schools down the road with our taxes! Still it's our choice and we don't regret it.'

They are happy to pay extra for all three children to have music lessons, even though they themselves are not musical: 'We just enjoy music, and think it very important. In any case, they get such pleasure out of it.' Wendy's parents, who are both very quiet, joke that they cannot imagine from where their children take their 'cleverness'.

But Janet adds seriously: 'My parents were very clever, and I think my mother was very disappointed that I was not at all clever. I remember that feeling so well. That is why I have never tried to push my children.'

They are proud that both their daughters gain excellent marks in their school exams, although David Moor sees just one small objection to the record of academic achievement: 'Wendy, for example, is a worrier. She is apprehensive about her work, although she won't say so. In a way I would like to see her more happy-go-lucky. . . . I think that perhaps she has felt there is pressure on her because of winning a scholarship. If it wasn't for her music, there would be no relaxation for her.'

Wendy: 'I've thought of doing archaeology as a career, though I don't really know. I've always been interested in fossils and old buildings – preserving things. This is in fact a prehistoric site you're on at this moment – under our house. In Victorian times apparently, when people were going for walks up here, they used to find lots of flints, and they picked them up. Then quite recently I found something in the garden, and thought, This looks like the tip of a spearhead or something. I see them in museums. Daddy said, Throw it over the hedge, it doesn't look like anything, but I kept it. And daddy was digging up the hedge and he found this long blade-thing which looked prehistoric, so somebody suggested we went to Norwich museum. So we took them in, and mummy produced the little arrowhead, and he said, Yes, that's an arrowhead.'

Then she produced the blade out of her bag, and he pounced on it, and said, 'Where did you get this from?' As Wendy is telling this story she is more animated than at any other time. 'They identified it – it was very exciting. So this is a prehistoric site. The man from the museum came to look and said it is very suitable, being on top of a hill. You can see for miles, you know. You can see the marshes, and you are supposed to be able to see the lights of nine towns. He said – flinty ground and the river; water and fishing; and they could see their enemies. Perfect. And some Roman things were found in a field down the road. One of them was a child's bulla – you know, those things children used to wear. It was a gold band and a sort of pouch and they wore them till they were about twelve, I think. They were removed as a sign of growing up and put in the family shrine forever. . . .'

Whilst her friends go off to play hockey, Wendy walks along the corridor of the music wing, and up the stairs to the practice rooms – rows of them, each one with double doors and a piano, each side of a long corridor. She takes her cello from the cupboard where the instruments are stored and waits outside one of the small music teaching rooms for her cello teacher to arrive. The lessons cost an extra £20 per term, with the same cost for singing and for piano.

Wendy says, 'It's a lot. Particularly as Susie does flute and piano, too, and Christopher does piano. It all adds up. I don't know how they manage, really. One has to make the most of lessons. I haven't really got a voice for singing. I'm just having them to help the cello – because drawing a bow is very like taking a breath, and it's very helpful.'

Mrs Nicholson arrives, carrying her own cello. They sit together in the small room, their backs to the bleakly beautiful view across the marshes, both concentrating, both listening intently to the sounds Wendy makes. She plays extremely well, face set, staring at her music. It is Bach's 'Ariosto'. When she has finished Mrs Nicholson launches into a long and detailed analysis of her playing; then they try again — the piano and cello in harmony; the long, compassionate notes filling the room as the sky loses its light.

'Right, that was fine. You should be able to play that to anyone and *enjoy* playing it. Now let's try "The Swan".'

They both turn the pages to find Saint-Saens — then once again the cello notes cut across the piano's cascade with slow precision. But Mrs Nicholson is not satisfied: 'I'll tell you what's the matter with that: when you're playing on the A string you do not have a straight bow. Give *each* one its fair share of the bow. . . . You've got to imagine very still water and a swan gliding over it. Play the scale of D major. . . . Now, were you satisfied with that?'

Wendy looks grave: 'No.'

'Well, try again. When you practise be *very* fussy. There's no point in doing it otherwise. . . . Now I know you have little time — you've too much to do, but try and practise as much as you can in the Christmas holidays.'

'I enjoy music, that's the main thing. It's my main relaxation. My orchy is on Saturday morning — it's the Norwich Students' Orchestra. Mummy or daddy drives me there, then they have to wait for me to bring me back. It's fun to play with other people — because there aren't that many good musicians at school. So I enjoy my orchy — I think I'd be swamped if I didn't have that. But music adds to the pressure on time. I'm up to Grade VIII on the piano now, and have a lesson in Southwold one evening a week.

'I try to listen to as much music as I can — we have lots of records. Mainly piano things and cello things. Listening to something like Dvořák makes me dream. . . . I sort of turn off completely and get involved in it. I think it takes some of the pleasure out of it to analyse it. I just like listening. It makes you think of things. . . . I'd love to be able to compose but I don't think I could. I'm not sure that I have musical ideas of my own in my head.'

A cold, foggy night. The road from Beccles to Norwich swirled with impenetrable mist, so that the fifteen miles had to be taken at a crawl. The Norwich Students' Orchestra was combining with the Norwich Comprehensive Schools' Choirs to give a festival of carols, sponsored by the Bible Society. It was held in St. Andrew's Hall, the nave of a group of buildings known as the Norwich Blackfriars. Wendy rushed home from school, ate hastily, changed into her long black skirt and white Victorian-style blouse, and joined Susie and her father for the long drive. She felt slightly nervous – as always when playing in front of an audience. But when she joined the crowds of school children in the lofty Blackfriars Hall, at the rear of St Andrew's Hall, she felt better. The choirs of four schools and the whole orchestra milled about the beautiful room, talking, laughing, admiring each other's appearance, taking instruments carefully from cases, tuning, practising a little, buzzing with excitement. The hall filled up. Wendy walked on to the platform with the rest of the orchestra, whilst the choirs massed behind them, distinguished by different coloured outfits. There was an air of celebration in the hall as choirs and audience bellowed 'Oh Come All Ye Faithful' accompanied by the orchestra.

Wendy concentrated, although she knew the familiar tune well: eyes fixed on her music; hair tied back as always into a low knot, looking critically at the choirs when they sang unaccompanied, noticing the weak notes. 'Noel Nouvelet', 'The First Nowell', 'The Shepherd's Cradle Song' ... the hall grew warmer and warmer, the singing louder and more relaxed. There was a feeling of Christmas in the room, of jollity.

When the Archdeacon of Norwich ascended the platform to give the address he identified it: 'Tonight as we enjoy these carols, we can begin for the first time to think that Christmas has really begun.... And I would like to ask you the question, Why do we celebrate Christmas? The answer comes from St Mark's gospel – we are celebrating the birth of the Son of Man, that is come to seek and to save that which is lost....'

Wendy had laid her cello back against her. She was staring out at the packed faces under the simple, vaulted wooden ceiling; then she looked back at the Archdeacon. Resonantly he reminded her, and the other children, and their assembled parents and teachers, of the inevitable, mysterious transformation at the root of their rejoicing: 'That infant Jesus that we sing of in the carols is become ... the Man of Sorrows.'

'I think I will go to university – although I don't actually *think* about it, you know. I would like to go. I couldn't stand to leave school and get a job in an office. I'd just hate being indoors, sitting doing the same thing every single day. I wouldn't be able to stand it. People do go to university out of interest, of course; that's part of it – if they're interested in a subject they want to find out more about it. But also to get a good job, a well-paid job that they don't find too boring. I think most people don't like their jobs. I can imagine what that must be like; but I can't imagine myself living in a sort of poky little flat in a town doing the same thing every day. . . .

'There's so many things to consider these days. I don't know. . . . There's more people doing wrong. It's harder to stay on the right sort of road. I mean, there are so many children that are criminals. There must be more pressure on them to do such awful things. Kill old ladies. . . . I remember reading about that. It was terrible. They see other people do it, and not just seeing other people doing it, but hearing of other people doing it; and thinking, Well, if they do it, it can't be that bad. They've nothing else to do; they're possibly just bored. Maybe no one to turn to. I mean, what *are* they going to do? There's nothing, is there?

'It's a combination of parents and teachers – mainly parents and your home background that influence you. You see, the people all around me have . . . sort of . . . been people who respect right, you know? They're sort of . . . nice. People who I get on with; my parents. I think you have to respect your children. And they've got to respect you – not exactly just obey you, but learn from you. But the parents have *got* to respect the children. We're human beings, aren't we? I think they can learn from children. Because children have a certain idea – their *own*. It hasn't been influenced by anyone else, not at first – when they are very little. When they get older, of course, it changes. Because of other people: what other people say, other people do. But in the beginning it's their own: this . . . *thing* in them. Oh, I don't know. But if children have been brought up to know bad things all the time, it's almost impossible for them to keep that. They are not going to know how to rebel against their parents and go the *right* way, are they? There are more children who rebel against the right things, and go the wrong way. Why? I suppose because they might be influenced by their friends. You need to be pretty strong-minded not to be.

'I never think of the future, really. Next year, in the sixth form, I suppose we'll feel more grown-up than we do now, but I don't think of it. I think you have to let yourself change gradually. I'm sort of mid-way. Everything is planned out for you when you're at school, and then you're suddenly grown-up and can suit yourself. At school there's a variety of things to do. When you leave school and get a job you're going to be doing the same sort of things all the time. That's your life. I don't know. . . . I don't know whether I want to grow up or not. I like being a child.'

12 Douglas

On the last Saturday of the year Douglas Sannachan walked round his city. Friday night had brought a blizzard: cars lay abandoned under their mounds of snow, and half the buses in the town had been withdrawn from the treacherous roads. Men tottered with their plastic bags of Bell's, Grouse and Haig, whilst the women stuffed still more selections of chocolates and crisps into their shopping bags, in readiness for the long holiday siege.

Hands in pockets he trudged from east to west, from the gaunt buildings of the Gallowgate, where he lives, to the bright shops along Argyle Street and Buchanan Street. Some shops already promised sales; in others plastic models preened in furs whose prices were secure. George Square was full of Christmas trees, coloured lights and offices for tourist information. He looked. Then, slipping and sliding, he returned through narrow side streets, past shops that grew shabbier, to Glasgow Cross, where the big clock would be watched the next midnight by his family from their living room window.

Douglas, whose friends all call him Sanny, turned into his own 'stair'. His home is in an old tenement building above some shops: a three-room flat on the fifth floor. He panted as he reached the top. His mother Nancy, his father William and his granny sat by the fire in the warm living room, with the television on. Nancy is thirty nine: small, dark and attractive; welcoming the visitor with a glass of scotch, cooking, cleaning, not worrying too much as long as her man is in work and her three children are out of trouble. Which they are: Louise is twenty one and has two children, nineteen-year-old Billy is engaged and working in the pie factory beside his dad; and Douglas has just left school at sixteen to be one of the lucky ones and find a job.

Once, though, Nancy became angry. Douglas tells how she was looking out of the window and saw, far below, two youths attacking an old man. She screamed and shouted that they should leave him alone, lied that he was her grandad, swore they should be ashamed. Her son, afraid they might come up, told her to be quiet. The youths ran off. It was not an occurrence which surprised either Douglas or his mother.

A newspaper lay on the sofa. Nancy showed it to her mother, shaking her head: 'Look at that picture . . . that laddie's scarred for life. And that's where Douglas was the night before. It could hae been him. I've told him not to go. . . .'

'Oh, ma!' said Sanny. The large photograph showed a sixteen-year-old boy's face, cut and stitched from earlobe to the corner of his mouth. He had been walking around the disco with his sister when, for no reason, he was slashed. 'It's pure chance,' said Sanny. 'You canna do anything about it.'

He left the house again, and cut through the streets to Glasgow Green. There the snow lay unbroken, and the People's Palace – Glasgow's museum and monument to its own working history – rose from a white, misty frosting. The bare trees wove a tracery above the path. 'It's magic, pure magic,' whispered Sanny, kicking up the sparkling powder with his black boots.

He was heading for the Dolphin Arts Centre, in James Street, Bridgeton. Douglas has spent all his life in the Calton and Bridgeton, in the East End of Glasgow – an area with some of the worst deprivation and strongest people in Europe. The people of Bridgeton suffer unemployment and alcoholism, poverty and crime: conditions as woven as the branches of those trees on Glasgow Green. Large areas now stand empty where the tenements used to be; but the Glasgow Eastern Area Renewal Scheme is attempting to bring back houses and jobs to the area, as well as those facilities necessary to a whole life – like parks, libraries, shops, markets and community centres – which other areas take for granted but which the people of Glasgow's East End have never had.

Douglas thinks it is about time. He shook the snow from his boots and sat in the warm office of the Dolphin Centre – the place he says has changed his life: 'I was born in the Calton – Claythorn Street. It's away now. Och, all the houses round there are away. We lived there when I was wee, then we moved to Barrowfield. It's bloody terrible down there, man – it's all gangs and things like that. It's kinda new; it's old but it's new, if you know what I mean – twenty-five to thirty years old. There's nuthin' there – there's nae shops there. No way. They've had to take all the shops away and the pubs because they kept getting broken into. It's the environment you're livin in, y'know? I mean I lived there about seven years, and in the first few years it was OK because there were shops and that down the London Road. But then they had to close all the shops, and the bread factory kept getting broken into – you'd get guys comin' to the door asking if you wanted to buy bread. And the people would go to Bridgeton to do their shopping. The house – our house – got broken into five times in one year. It was people we knew. That's bad that, people you know breaking into your ain house. The telly went – my mother's still paying it off. It was a brand new one, up to date. She thought she was doing well – she loved it. And the house was beautiful, but it got broken into a good few times, and it ruined her, y'know.

'I lived there from when I was five or six to when I was about twelve. When I was five and six it was a great place because there was hundreds of wee weans running about. When I was in Calton I was wee so I dinna remember but it was all tenement buildings. But Barrowfield was a new place – oh, new houses, and that's gonna be great. . . . And it was at first, it was smashing. But then as you get older, the gangs grow. All the weans I knew, all the young lads were growing up to knives. They were all fighting. That's what it's like – it's pure war, I'm telling you. They've got guns and that down there. To survive you've got to be in a gang. You've got to be hard and tough and all that. There's murders. Puff (he's my friend) was living there until a few days ago. His mother got mugged. We were going up the stair and she came up after us, and we were shouting Hallo, and she looked up and – och, her face was all blood. I was shattered. She was crying, My new glasses, my new glasses, what's your dad gonna say? That's what she was worried about. Puff said, If I find out who it was, mammy, I'm gonna murder him. That happened six months ago.

'All the wee weans, that size,' he raises his hand about four feet from the ground, 'they're all runnin' about fighting. There's the Spur and the Young Spur. And there's the Torch. They're famous in Barrowfield. They're bad bastards, so they are, pure evil. You've never met such evil people in your life. They go about just choppin' guys up for nothing. It makes me sick, I'm telling you. Doin' guys in, for nothing. Just come up and chib you, slash you in the face. Once, I was only about seven or eight, and I got a fascination with this cleaning machine – this lorry that comes up the street, with brushes that turn round. It was magic, I thought it was brilliant, and I was walking up the street after it, and I ended up at the top of the street in Torchland. That's the gang's territory, y'know? I knew for a fact that I shouldnae have been up there, but I got so involved with this machine that I did. . . . And this guy came up with a razor and just went like that [makes quick side to side movements with his hands] right across my face. Waaaah – blood! I ran down the road calling for me ma . . . and me ma wasnae in. So I had to go round to the woman next door – Mrs Kelly. She said, Ohh, come in, laddie. . . .

'Och, they've got shotguns and all up there. Once these guys poured lighter fuel on me and set me on fire, but I put it out all right. It happens all the time, things like that. See these wee scars on my face?

'It all goes back to the environment – there's nothing to do. They all stand about the corners, and sometimes if they've money they go off and get drunk. It makes it worse for them. And maybe their mothers and fathers make it worse for them. And maybe they've got no money. So the guys'll go and break into a shop. And they think it's all part of being a big man: they've gotta prove they're hard. I think you've got to be tough to live about here. That's what *they* think anyway. But if you use your head there's no need to be like that.

'My mother and father wanted to leave Barrowfield because of what it was like, and the house being broken into. We moved back to Calton and my ma, she loves it now. Och, we stay in an old tenement and there's nae hot water. We've nae got a bath or anything like that. And the kitchen ceiling's fallen down on my ma's head twice now. My dad pulled her out of the way in time. And we've mice running around. But it's nae a bad house. It disnae bother me. I still sleep with my big brother. We pull the settee down in the kitchen. My ma and dad sleep in the bedroom and just now my granny's staying with us on the couch in the living room.

'If I got into a fight and came home, my dad would say, Did you get him? Did you get him back? That's all. Because my dad's a Calton boy himself – he knows what it's like. He was brought up in Calton and Bridgeton. He was a Teddy Boy – he does all the Elvis stuff. Garbage! My ma was from Hamilton – she was a foreigner. She's a fantastic singer – pure magic, man. They're great.

'My ma and dad went to Blackpool for the Scottish weekend once. They said they were drunk all the time . . . drunk on the way down and on the way back! They've never been on a good holiday.

'I've never been on a good holiday – till I went on tour with the youth theatre last year.' He laughs. 'Och, I went to Saltcoats and Stevensen – everybody goes there. It's a seaside place near Glasgow. It was great. . . . My grandad and granny were members of this Navy club, and the club used to put on bus rides, and all the weans could go, and we'd go to the seaside, and have races in the sand: sack races, and egg-and-spoon races. It was magic. I was about ten. I'd be speaking to my mates, and some of them would say, We went to Blackpool; We went to Cardiff; We went to Butlins; and I'd say, I went to Saltcoats. Brrrrr [blows a raspberry] Saltcoats! They might have had more money – or maybe their mothers and fathers had just saved up for a good holiday. I don't know. It didnae worry me.

'It was great just getting away from school. I'd just run about the streets. We'd our own wee gang and all . . . it wasnae a fightin' gang . . . well, maybe it was, we used to fight with the other classes.

'I hated school, couldn't stand it. It was just like being out on the street – there were guys walking about all the time, annoying you. Fighting. Every time the police walked past the playground every-body would shout: Funny police, they're all barm-pots. Once all these police horses came past and they was all shouting, and about seven police horses came right round, through the car park and into the school. *You*, you, *you*, and you – come here. The headmistress nearly cracked up. At school all the guys were neds – hard men – tough guys. Y'know, hundreds of buttons up their sleeves, and big coats with pockets for all their blades.

'The teachers mean well, but the young ones take the piss out of them. But they're hell of hard teachers in there. We had a music teacher, he was brilliant, but these wee guys took a lend o' him: I'm away sir; Where are you going? To the toilet – and they didnae come back. I've done it myself. I liked doing the school pantomime. The first year I was there my brother was in it, and the next year I got a part. And the next year I got a bigger part. I loved it, so I did, man.

'When I got into the fourth year I thought it was brilliant. But the thing is, you're a wee guy, and the neds are running about and they put pressure on you because they don't want to learn anything anyway. They were only at school for a carry-on. It's not so much the pressure. . . . I mean – I'm just watching them and I'm gonna do what they're doing, aren't I? I ended up not listening. It was all a big daft carry-on to me. But I loved school in the fourth year. I loved woodwork. I made a table, but it got broke last week. My big brother broke it. It was a great table and all.

'I don't like teachers being like teachers. I like them to be one of the group like equal. Like women being equal to men. Only . . . all being part of the group. One of *us*. . . . Everybody being the one person. See, at school, they're blabbering things out and writing them up on the board and you're supposed to take all that in. But your mind wanders. It's boring. Same old things every day.

'I don't think it could have been different. I mean . . . that's how
it is. You ask a young guy, about twelve, thirteen, if they like
school and they'll say 'no' – because it'll be the same as it was for me.
Same all the time. But once they realize, when they're older and
leaving school, once they realize that it matters – they'll wish they'd
done more. But there *are* the ones that stick in at school . . . they
got O-levels. But I didnae. My mind was all over the place. I fell
asleep once in my primary school, and the next thing I knew was
. . . whack . . . the belt, y'know? Chasing me round the class. Big
leather thing – cuts you. Some teachers don't like using it, but they
all do. . . . Those guys that worked, they got the piss taken out of
them all the time. But when an exam come up it was all best friends
– How's it going, Jimmy? Sit next to me in the exam. Then after –
Aagh you, yer toffy . . . all that. It's hard for guys like that – they
take a hell of a lot of beating. But at the end all the other ones were
pure jealous. They knew they wouldnae get O-levels. They knew
they wouldnae get anywhere – like me. Me clever? You kiddin? No
way. I wish I was. Just to know a wee bit mair. Me, I couldnae read
a book – just get bored with it after a while. I'll read a play we're
doing at the youth theatre but that's different.

'I loved music. I thought it was brilliant. I was never out of music
class. Fantastic. I learned to read music and all that. I like playing
an instrument and I like listening to anything . . . any music at all,
from classical to punk rock. My friends and family, they don't like
classical music, I dinna know why. Oh *no*! And 'cos I've been coming down the Dolphin they think, Och, he's different – he's listening to classical music! But I've liked it since I was in first year at
school. I just enjoyed the sound of strings, violins and cellos and all
that. At Christmas there was an opera thing on the telly, but my ma
said, Oh, that's garbage; put it off.

'Why didn't I stay on at school? It was all a matter of money. The
likes of me . . . see, I wanted to stay on at school, and I says to
myself, Am I going to work hard this time, or am I just going to go
there for a carry-on? My mother said, Aye, you could stay on, but I'd
rather you didnae. She wanted me to go out to work. It would have
been nice to stay one . . . she would have liked it in a way, but the
money wasn't coming in. My ma was keeping me; my dad did have a
job then, but my big brother was unemployed, y'know? So I says,
No. Bugger it – I'll go out and work. But I've no regretted leaving
school, because I'm in work and I love my work just now. Well, in a
way I have regretted it because I loved it at the end, but if I'd stayed
in I'd liked to have worked somewhere like the Dolphin in the end –

community worker. I just like people, like talking to people. Qualifications, aye. If I'd got any mair – if I'd got my English, I might have stayed on. But I only just passed my music. I didnae work.

'I left in the summer. Then the Dolphin had this big Festival of Fun parade, and there was a dance. And we got posters to distibute all round Bridgeton to tell people about it. So I was taking them round to works and asking if they'd display a poster, and then I'd say, By the way, any jobs? And they'd say no.

'Then I was really lucky because I went into Thomas Graham's and I says, Can I speak to personnel? And the lassie says, Yes, just in there. So I go into the woman and I say – I put on a posh accent and that – Could you please display these posters? and she says, Oh, certainly. I gave her the posters and then I said, Oh, by the way, any jobs? And she says, Aye, as a matter of fact there is – as a warehouseman. It's like a big building trade merchants, y'know? So I said, Great – have you got an application form? So she gave it to me and I went down the road and wrote it out, then took it back. And she says, Can you come back tomorrow and meet the manager? 'cos she seemed to like the application. So I came down to meet the manager and he asked me to spell this word – I'd wrote it down on the application form and I'd spelt it wrong. So I spelt it right when I said it. And he goes, It's funny that the kids nowadays (and I *hated* that, when he said kids) they can't write things down, but they can spell. So then he said, OK, we'll start you Monday, and aaah, I was over the moon!

'I thought I was a big man. I was sitting in the house saying, I've got a job, I've got a job. I was sitting down relaxing and my ma was giving me cups of tea. I usually make my ain tea! And she said, I'll make pieces up, and I thought, Ohhh, my dad gets pieces [sandwiches]. And the first day it was spam and egg. And I was walking to work and I thought, Oh, this is going to be fantastic.

'I can remember my first day at work, every inch. I went in the big gate, and I was dead early. It was only half past seven and I didnae start until eight! I was worried, y'know – a bit worried about meeting all these big *men*! I was sitting there and this guy came in. said, My name's Sanny – Dougie Sannachan. He says, Are you starting here? I says, Aye, I'm starting today. And he says, Och that's good. And this was the time of the World Cup, y'know? So says, Did you see the game last night – Scotland? I had to try and start up a conversation! He says, Aye, fuckin' rubbish, wasn't it? and I says, aye. Phew – I was sweatin'! I didnae know what to do. I wa dead quiet. And he said, What y'doing? Are you going to work in the office or the warehouse? I said, It's a warehouse job. And he said, You'd better get they clothes off, anyway. I had dress trousers on . . . not my new ones, but had to look kind of smart for my first day in work. And we walked in through this big steel door and the guys was all sitting up on the benches and they all scarpered when Harry walked in and started working away!

'It's a big warehouse with a trade counter. We sell things – like valves, and pipes, and everything. I can't serve at the counter yet 'cos I'm not grade one, so I'm out the back, lifting things and making things up for the postal service to go out in the van, and all that. I dinna wear an overall yet. But we're getting them. . . . The union cracked up because we needed new ones. And we was all out in the yard – this was my first union meeting. It was frozen. And he says, If we're not going to get any suitable clothing for this cold weather we're out on strike tomorrow. And that was the day before Christmas Eve, so I thought, What's the point of that? But I thought, I'm a big man – at a union meeting. Just like my dad. I'm not in the union yet, by the way, I'm getting my form. Transport and General Workers.

'They keep you busy at work, I enjoy it. Sometimes it's real interesting. I'm reading this book right now . . . because later on I'll sit a test. . . . It shows you how to build a house. And they give you a discount on anything you want to buy, like wallpapers and paint from the other departments. The guys I work with are good guys – we're forever getting a laugh. I talk away about the Dolphin and they're all real interested and that! John – he's the union man – says to me, That's our thespian. And I says, What's a thespian? He says, You should know what that is, boy. And they kid me on that doing all that acting and that, I must be bent, queer, y'know? They're only carrying on. I hope they're only carrying on, anyway. I couldnae stand it if they thought it was true. Ugh, that's horrible.

'Och aye, I like work. But no way will I do it for the rest of my life. I'll get bored with it after a while, I know I will. I've been doing it seven months now. Started June. I get £28 a week – that's before stoppages. I give my ma a tenner a week. I leave at half past seven and take my pieces. I hate getting up in the morning. My ma's screaming her head off. I canna hear her.

'The people round here have fun when they go for a drink on a Friday. That's their idea of enjoyment. It isnae really mine. My idea of enjoyment is watching other people enjoy me performing – working at it. Even in work I do that – have a carry-on. But even in work

... och, man, it gets a bit boring. Aye. Sometimes you get worked off your feet and you feel like cracking up. Sometimes I get bored, if there's nothing happening.

'Saturday night and it's pure boredom. That's when I get depressed. So I end up going to the pictures or something by myself. It just happens now and again. Sometimes it's seeing the same people, and going tae the same places. And birds ... they hang about you all the time. I get bored. Birds. ... Sometimes they don't interest me at all – I had my first bird when I was about fifteen. It's nice while you're doing it, but I wouldn't go looking for it, if you know what I mean. Pure boredom. I know guys that slap their birds about. I don't think that's right – I wouldnae slap a bird about. That's just another excuse to be big. We had this party last night. It was good – we were dancing and singing songs and enjoying ourselves. But there was nae birds. You gotta get off with a bird ... but it's no just a matter of getting off with a bird, you've gotta enjoy yourself, too. I mean I don't fancy going to a party and getting off with a bird and then sitting with her all evening. Sitting around winchin'. It's necessary ... but it would be great to have a bird at the end of the night when everything's quiet and everyone's steamin' and the lights are down and someone's put an LP on, and you sit winchin' with your bird. Snoggin', in other words.

'The guys start running round with the gangs at about thirteen or fourteen, and then about fifteen-sixteen they want tae get some birds, and then when they're about eighteen they want tae get married. I couldnae do that. It's just a constant routine like a production line all the time: eat, sleep, work, drink, eat, sleep, work, drink. And sex – all that garbage, man. Marriage is just an excuse to be in bed with a bird all the time. Garbage. I don't fancy getting married. Stopping with the same old bag all my life. You can divorce and all that but round about here they just stick each other out. There's always fights. Everywhere – all the mas and the das and the uncles and the aunts – fighting. It's just this ... *thing*. There's always got to be a fight ... or an argument. It always happens. Somebody says the wrong thing. That's it.

'I started smoking at fourteen. I couldn't tell my ma and dad – my dad would boot me and tell me it was bad for me – coughing away himself! But he disnae mind now. 'Cos I'm working. Once you're working you're a man, a *man*. Och, I was born when I was twenty-two ... that's why I hate being called a kid – it reminds me of being a wee wean.

'I like getting older. I'm enjoying life just now – it's fantastic.

I'm watching Bridgeton get built up again, y'know. For a while it was pure dead, with nothing happening. I like seeing it built up, and I'm joining in. I like doing things with the youth theatre – we perform for the people. And there's arts and crafts markets and all that. I enjoy watching people enjoy us, if you know what I mean. I like seeing people enjoy themselves, because they get that much pressure on them.

'A lot of press have been writing bad things about Bridgeton – about the alcoholics and the fighting and everything. I don't really blame anybody, y'know. What can you do? The East End is certainly deprived, but I don't know who to blame. I'm not really political at all. The people in Bridgeton and Barrowfield are trying to do what they can to help each other, but it's the young ones. . . . See, if they could just get into the swing of things and try to help each other I think it would be great – it would be magic. But it's all a matter of being a big man – that makes them the evil way. I've never been a big man. I was soft. I was a wee shakebag, a wee feary. I couldnae protect myself, y'know? So I gave all the guys a laugh – they thought I was pure mad. I was doing that just to show I was different. I think they'd like to be like me and go down the Dolphin Centre, but it would ruin their pride – being hard men.

'I just used to stay in the house before I came down here. See – I was at John Street, my secondary school, and in the third year you get leisure – you get an afternoon off each week to do what you like. Well, nae what you like – they give you specific things to choose from, like cookery, PE, all that. There was photography and making puppets. And you thought, Making puppets! Fuck! That's for weans, and all that. But I thought, Och, I'll dae it, and Puff did too. Just two of us out of the whole year. Och, it didnae matter. So we had to come down here, the Dolphin, for that. Then we started to come down nights, and maybe dinner time, come in and see wee John, the janitor. And one night I was standing outside with this lassie I was going with, and we were talking, and I was totally pissed off – Ohh, she's rubbish and this is pure boredom – and there wasnae much happening. And this guy comes out, he was the stage manager and he's worked with us with the puppets, and he says, Sanny, you want to go on a tour in your summer holidays – doing drama and all that? So I says, Aye, man, anything for a laugh. So I went in and I got to know the people who run the youth theatre. Aye, it's completely changed my life. 'Cos I'd probably have ended up knocking off motors, too.

'Puff and me, we came into the Dolphin and we liked it, and we thought, Och, we'll be different, we'll come here all the time. Because it's a really good place and we really enjoy it. We never actually said, We'll be different; it was never a conscious thing. But other people are making out that we *are* different. 'Cos we are *different*!

'At first I thought my ma and dad thought I was daft coming to the Dolphin. I'd be in the house and me dad would say, Want to go and see Rangers and Celtic? and I'd say, No, dad, I'm going down to the Dolphin. And he'd go like that [frowns] – That's no my boy. You know: Who is he? He's no real. But now they all like me coming down here because they know I'm not going to get into any trouble.

'It's depressing round here to see all the people drunk. You see old men walking along the street – pure steaming. I think that's terrible. But when I do it, it's different! And round here we got a bad name because of the religion as well. They're still into all that. I know a woman who's a right bluenose. She wouldnae wear anything green. It's fucking sickening, so it is, man, it's a hell of a Protestant area, round here. Last year this Canadian band was coming over for this massive walk and they put up all these decorations, wee triangles and coloured lights in the streets. And they don't even do that at Christmas. Just because it was an Orange march – bloody great Union Jacks everywhere. I'd love to see all that at Christmas, but they don't do anything at Christmas. The nearest they got to nice bright lights round here was on the lemonade factory – they put up a big tree with lights. . . . That's the nearest we got to it round here. With all the houses empty and the people away and the old men walking about the streets. . . .

'But it comes back to pride. That's what you forget about. People round here have their pride. It might be all they've got, by the way. See, if you ask me what does it look like from my point of view, I'll say, It's a dead nice place. Kids are running round knocking off motors and cutting each other, but the *people* – the people round here are really good, y'know? So they are. There's this new thing – GEAR – Glasgow Eastern Area Renewal – and they're building new houses, and the houses are going to be run by the community. It's a project thing. And they (i.e. GEAR) got this money from the Strathclyde Council to build these wee pretty gardens . . . and the old winos sit looking at them. Then the women say they don't want tae go there because the old winos go. I don't know. . . . It dinna do much good to make wee gardens when there's nae houses, but it's a new thing. I don't know. . . .'

'I'm enjoying myself just now seeing Bridgeton built up. I'd like to see it made into a better place for the people that stay here. I'm proud of it, so I am. I was going wi' a lassie from the south and I wanted her to come up, but her dad wouldnae let her. I was fucking mad – cracked up. I'm proud – because I've got to live in the place, haven't I? It's no the way it looks, it's the people in it. You get the villains everywhere. OK – so there's the bad houses and Glasgow's a bad city. Howl! I don't care. I like it.

'And New Year, man, it's magic. They don't do much in the south, do they? But up here it's great. It's one big party because it's the time the people enjoy themselves. In our house, the New Year party's just one big rabble rabble. Everybody talks at once. But when somebody gets up to sing, everybody's quiet. At New Year I feel glad if it's been a bad year. Glad it's over. But if it's been a good year you feel dead sad. This year's been a good year for me. Because of the youth theatre, and even because leaving school and working's been good. It's been completely different this year, man. Because all the other years have been the same . . . all the other years of my life. It's been different since I started coming to the Dolphin. I can't remember one thing that happened before that. Everything was the same and I never took anything in. Never. Things around me, things that's happening . . . so this year is different. It's much better than what it was, and I hope next year is good. I hope we can get some money at the Dolphin to make a film.

'I've always wanted to be in a film. On the silver screen, y'know!' He laughs at himself. 'It's dead exciting – acting. Seeing an audience; just being with the youth theatre. We go to the Citizens' Theatre sometimes – on the free nights. The free nights are fantastic 'cos there's all the weans from the Gorbals screaming and shouting. It's magic. Things like that are important to people – och aye, *definitely*. They *need* things – they need to enjoy themselves like that. We had film shows in the Dolphin for the old people, old movies.

'I'd love to work in here, so I would. I could teach people puppetry . . . because I love talking to people. It's no as if I'd have to be a big teacher – I'd be part of a group. Because I treat everything as a group. I love being in a group of people, all working together. That's how I'd like to see Bridgeton, you know? It's been treated as a bad place and it *was* a bad place but it could be better. I wouldnae move . . . well, I'd like a bigger house with my ain room, and that, but *in* Bridgeton. But I'd love to move away every now and again and get away. Maybe get a travelling job. See new places. Meet new people . . . like your kind of job, I'd love that. But I haven't got the brains for that kind of thing. I know. But it would be magic.

'People have said to me, Why d'ye no go in for the drama college? I'd love to get into the drama college but ... I don't know. I'm gonna try, I think. You do a wee audition. You take a scene from a play you've done and just do it. It depends how good you are. You don't need O-levels for the drama course. Och, I don't know. I think maybe I'll try. But I don't know if I could do anything like that.'

That night Sanny went to a party, walking perilously through snow and ice. He didn't enjoy it: 'Nae lassies again. And a load of neds standing around saying, Who's he?.' But Sunday was 'nearday' – the day before New Year, and like everyone else he grew excited. Nancy spent all day scouring the house of every scrap of dirt, making ready for the family party, whilst William surveyed the ranged bottles of spirits with satisfaction. There seemed enough to drink to last a week – lots of ice in the fridge, the records piled by the new 'music centre', the ornaments arranged at regular intervals on the mantelpiece and shelves, the potatoes ready peeled in the pan for the first meal of the New Year.

When it grew dark Sanny went out for a walk, breathing in the expectation with the bitter cold. He passed an old man lying in a doorway, who raised a feeble hand for help. 'OK, Jimmy, OK,' he panted, heaving him to his feet, and leaning him back against the wall. The old man swayed. 'He's pure steamin' already,' grinned Sanny, turning back towards home.

His cousins, Douglas, Iris, Alan and Frankie arrived, with Uncle Dougie and Aunt Jessie, and the kids sat and watched television whilst Nancy, William, Dougie and Jessie went up the road to the Moon Inn – open for a couple of hours for a 'Scottish Night' to celebrate Hogmanay. The heaters did not work, the breaths of the drummer and organist showed in white clouds – but Nancy stood at the mike and sang 'Scotland the Brave' and 'Keep Right on Till the End of the Road' in her beautiful, belting voice. When the call came everyone stood up, crossed hands and sang 'Auld Lang Syne' – wet-eyed already, though it was only 9.30.

They panted and laughed loudly as they ascended the stair – cracking jokes so fast no club comedian could match them: Uncle Dougie with his patter and Jessie with her cackling laugh, and all the vodka inside them. At home, Sanny and his cousins had been joined by his big sister Louise, her husband Vick, and her two children Andrew and Vicky. Louise left school at sixteen to have Andrew; eighteen-month-old Vicky is the pet of the whole family. She wandered around the room, offering each adult a crisp on her tiny outstretched palm: '*Thank you*, hin. She's a clever girl; she's *such a clever girl!*' Vicky stared round the room at them all, at the glasses on the table, and the smiling faces perched around on arms of chairs and stools.... 'Kiss, kiss, Vicky – gie us a kiss.' Big hands grabbed her, hoisting her against a wide chest. 'Come to your grandad ... she's mine; are ye your grandad's, hin?' A smell of whisky and tobacco.

Ten, ten-thirty, eleven. Nancy and William danced to 'Mama's got a Squeezebox', while Sanny jogged his granny round the floor. Glasses were emptied and filled. Jessie went through the kitchen for more ice – where her children Alan and Iris were attempting to keep Andrew quiet. But he ran through to look for his mother, big, tough Louise, who frowned and put down her cigarette and her glass: 'Wait, Andrew, *wait!*' Then she held out her arms, and he curled into her, resting his head on her ample chest. Nancy smiled: 'That's all he was wanting – a cuddle from his mammy.'

Sanny said: 'He's pure spoilt – look at him.' But Louise was frowning and kissing her son, as if the frown might disguise the feeling. 'That's what they're here for – the weans. Spoiling. Aren't you, pal? *Aren't* you? They'll get none of it later on.'

Vicky was sitting on William's lap, emptying an old purse filled specially for her with a few old foreign coins. 'Mon – ey,' she chanted, her eyes open wide.

William looked up and said, to no one in particular: 'See, the lassies are trained from birth to do the shopping. The wean's interested in the purse and the money. They're bred to it. It's the way it is.'

But his sister-in-law Jessie derided him from across the room: 'And why don't the men have that training, that's what I want to know? 'You know what you can do with your training!' They all laughed – as the music grew louder, as Nancy bobbed around the room, and the cigarette smoke rose in a cloud to the ceiling.

Eleven-thirty. Nancy disappeared into the kitchen to start the food. It was nearly time. Uncle Dougie had put the television on and was smiling and tapping his feet to the massed strings playing Scottish music.

'All the weans have got to be in the front room for the bells,' panted Nancy, rushing through to make sure everybody had a full glass.

'You see,' whispered Sanny, 'at twelve all the bells of Glasgow ring, and it's the New Year. It's magic, man, so it is.'

Five-year-old Andrew was looking tired and bad-tempered, but

Nancy, his young grandmother, encouraged him with her own excitement: 'Soon it'll be time for the bells, and then we'll have a kiss. . . .'

Not long. Seven adults and five children, and Sanny and his sixteen-year-old cousin Douglas, who would not call themselves children, but whom their parents would not call adults – all clustered together, waiting. Ten to twelve. Five to twelve. Wait. A minute to go. . . .

Bonnnnnnng. Bonnnnnnng. . . . The reverberations from the clock tower at Glasgow Cross broke the tension. Nancy and William embraced and everybody kissed everybody else, in an elaborate and careful ritual – crossing the room, repeating, 'Happy New Year' with warmth. No one could be missed, not even thirteen-year-old Iris, who had moaned that she 'hated all that kissing'. Nancy and Jessie went into the kitchen to finish the important, symbolic first meal . . . reappearing with plates of steak and kidney pie, mashed 'tatties' and peas.

As Sanny sat and forked his food eagerly into his mouth he said: '*Now* I can say I'm seventeen *this year*. It's fantastic. Do you think it's a good party? Do you think we have good New Years? Och, but this New Year it's different for me. Different to the ones that's gone before. I'm drinking in front of my ma and I'm smoking in front of my dad – for the first time like this at New Year, and they don't mind – 'cos I'm a man now and they're treating me like a man. Och, but they're great, my ma and dad. I know it sounds soft, and all that – but I love all my family, so I do.'

But by 2 a.m. he grew slightly bored. The party would go on until morning and all through the next day with all the children in his bed, and the adults taking turns to have a couple of hours' sleep in Nancy's bed.

Sanny wanted to go 'first-footing', and say Happy New Year to his best friend, Puff. His mother made sure he had some drink to take with him, and he walked through the streets, through Barrowfield, where he used to live, past Bridgeton Cross, to the new high-rise blocks of flats. As he approached the estate, he paused: 'Listen.' And from scores of lighted windows came the faint sound of party music and distant laughter.

The lift smelt slightly of urine. 'Puff's having a party – it'll be just young people like me. It'll be very different to how it was at home,' said Sanny, banging on the door. Sure enough – the room was dim, the music quiet, and a couple sat on the sofa with their mouths glued together. Whilst three or four couples danced and draped over each other, Sanny sat drinking beer with his closest friends, Puff and Rab, talking more and more quickly, laughing more and more loudly. The three boys agreed that their discovery of the Dolphin Arts Centre came at a crucial time: instead of leaving school, Puff had stayed on, and Rab had started a stage management course. But Sanny looked, for a fraction of a second, disconsolate.

Rab turned to him: 'You should do what I'm doing, Sanny. Or do anything else. You'll nae stay doing that job you're in. It's monkey's work, Sanny; just work for monkeys.'

At 5 a.m. Sanny walked home. The cold streets were empty. Car windows were thick with ice, and even the sounds of far-off revelry had ceased. His feet crunched through the snow as he walked back through the gloomy decaying buildings of Barrowfield and across the open spaces where the houses used to be. He stopped – a small figure in the moonlight, and looked around at a landscape made indistinct by the snow.

'That's where I used to stay – the stair was right there,' pointing at the empty snow.

'That was my first school over there – it was a great school, too, pointing at the dark and shuttered building where no children have talked in class for years.

'And over there, in that corner, that's where the most horrible thing, the most *horrible* thing I've ever known, happened to me. It was fucking terrible, and for years I wouldn't talk about it. But it disnae matter now; I'm not a wean any mair. It was when I was a wee wean – I don't know how old. Five. Six. And I was playing out behind the close. And all these big guys came chasing me, and they took all my clothes. And I remember being *cold*. Then I just passed out. And I remember coming round and seeing all these . . . faces . . . just looking at me. Staring above me. With nae clothes. And my mammy and my daddy came and took me in. . . . That's all it was, but it was the most horrible thing. I've never forgotten it, and it used to make me feel terrible to think of being there like that – helpless. Horrible. I dinna know what effect that sort of thing has on your mind. . . .' He pointed at a broken wall and the frost sparkling upon it.

He walked past the huge billboard where kids from the Dolphin and a local youth club had painted a mural on the back; it was a sequence of surreal images drawn by a Glasgow artist and carefully painted in. Sanny stared at it: 'It's magic. Look at it. The more you look at it, the more you can see. And all the different bits mean different things each time you look at them. . . . This thing's been up for a couple of years now, and see, no one's touched it. No spray-cans. The word got round. The older guys told the young ones, Leave that alone — we done that. They think it's great.'

Sanny looked exasperated once more. 'It's what's *needed*. More things like that. Things they can *do*.... Och, but they mightnae do them. They might not like the things I like. I can only speak for myself. See, my dad grew up in these streets, and so did my brother Billy and so did I. And we're all supposed to be the same. All the boys of Calton grew up the same as their dads and do the same things. I'm not the same as my big brother. But I'm supposed to be. Yet, I *am* the same as him, too, if y'know what I mean. I *am* the same. The job I do is the same. My family is the same.... But I don't want to be the same. (Now I know I'm pure steaming just now — well, no steaming, I can walk straight!) But I do.... I want to *make* something of my life.'